The Blue Max Airmen
German Airmen Awarded the Pour le Mérite
Volume 1
Boelcke & Immelmann

Lance J. Bronnenkant, PhD.

The Blue Max Airmen
German Airmen Awarded the Pour le Mérite
Volume 1
Boelcke & Immelmann
Lance J. Bronnenkant, PhD.

Interested in WWI aviation? Join The League of WWI Aviation Historians (www.overthefront.com) and Cross & Cockade International (www.crossandcockade.com)

© 2012 Aeronaut Books, all rights reserved
Text © 2012 Lance J. Bronnenkant, PhD.
Design and layout: Jack Herris
Cover design: Aaron Weaver
Aircraft Colors and Markings: Greg VanWyngarden
Color Profiles: Jim Miller
Digital photo editing: Aaron Weaver & Jack Herris
Printed in USA by Walsworth Publishing Company

Aeronaut Books

www.aeronautbooks.com

Publisher's Cataloging-in-Publication data

Bronnenkant, Lance J.
   The Blue Max Airmen: German Aviators Awarded the Pour le Mérite: Volume 1 / by Lance J. Bronnenkant.
   p. cm.
   ISBN 978-1-935881-05-6
1. Boelcke, Oswald, 1891–1916. 2. Immelmann, Max, 1890–1916. 3. World War, 1914–1918 --Aerial operations, German. 4. Fighter pilots --Germany. 5. Aeronautics, Military -- Germany -- History. II. Title.

ND237 .S6322 2011
759.13 --dc22   2011904920

Table of Contents

The Orden Pour le Mérite	4
Oswald Boelcke	
The Man	7
The Aircraft	32
Military Service & Victory List	60
Max Immelmann	
The Man	62
The Aircraft	86
Military Service & Victory List	102
Pour le Mérite Winners by Date of Award	104
Pour le Mérite Winners Alphabetically	105
Index	106
Bibliography & Glossary	109
Color Section	
Profile Captions	111
Color Profiles	Inside front & back covers

I would like to thank Josef Scott for his expert input on Fokker *Eindecker* aircraft.

– Lance J. Bronnenkant

Anthony Fokker's D.III prototype was given serial number 350/16 after its acceptance into military service. Oswald Boelcke tested this aircraft and later flew 352/16 that was quite similar in appearance (see pages 50–53).

The Orden Pour le Mérite

The *Orden Pour le Mérite* (Order for Merit) was created by Friedrich the Great on 6 June 1740 as the highest award that Prussia could bestow upon an officer for bravery in the face of the enemy.[1] Friedrich, an admirer of France's language and court customs, often used French in an official capacity – hence the phrase *"pour le mérite"* in his new decoration's title. The medal consisted of a gold Maltese cross with blue enamel filling in the arms (front and reverse). On the face of the enamel, in gold, were a crowned "F" signifying Friedrich the Great (top arm of the cross) and the words *"Pour"* (left arm), *"le Mé,,"* (right arm) and *"rite"* (bottom arm). Four gold eagles with outstretched wings were attached between the cross-arms. The "v" of the top Maltese cross-arm either had a baroque-style loop located toward its bottom or was mostly filled with a flat, semi-circular segment (or "pie-slice") that sported a hole in its upper portion. Fitted through the loop or "pie-slice" hole was an oblong suspension ring through which the order's ribbon passed. The ribbon was black with silver stripes near each edge. The *Pour le Mérite* was to be worn "at all times" (i.e., whenever in uniform), dangling from the tunic collar. A separate, higher grade, the *Orden Pour le Mérite mit Eichenlaub* (Order for Merit with Oakleaves) that added three clustered oak leaves to the suspension ring on the top cross-arm, was instituted in 1813; but since it was never bestowed upon a World War I aviator, no more will be said about it here.

During the first few years of World War I, the *Pour le Mérite* order was made of solid gold. Due to a shortage of precious metals, however, it was officially decreed on 16 November 1916 that it could instead consist of silver with a thin coating of gold ("silver-gilt"). At first, jewelers such as Wagner or Godet (Berlin) or Rothe (Vienna) appear to have had an official role in supplying the military. Yet as the war progressed – and particularly as recipients began to order second "wearer's copies" to preserve their original orders – smaller, private jewelers were commissioned to produce the medal as well. The result was a wide variety of *Pour le Mérite* versions exhibiting subtle differences in quality, style, detail, finish, size, weight and enamel hues.

The *Pour le Mérite* was a Prussian decoration, that is, technically issued by the independent Kingdom of Prussia. But by virtue of Wilhelm II's position as Kaiser and his practice of bestowing it upon men from all regions of Germany, it evolved into more of a national award. According to the late Neal O'Connor, 687 men were granted the *Pour le Mérite* by war's end.[2] The annual number of awards increased each year as the conflict, and perhaps Germany's need for publicly recognized heroes, progressed: 13 (1914), 56 (1915), 85 (1916), 177 (1917) and 356 (1918). Of these, a total of 81 (or 11.8%) went to individuals having a role in aviation: 57 army fighter pilots, 3 navy fighter pilots, 11 two-seater men, 5 bombing unit commanders, 2 airship commanders, 1 balloonist and 2 aviation staff officers. Though none of them were given out in 1914–15, their annual rate of increase mirrored the overall pattern thereafter: 13 (1916), 28 (1917) and 40 (1918). Clearly, the lion's share of aviation awards went to fighter pilots. In part, this was due to the more cut-and-dry standard established for their eligibility: the number of enemy aircraft shot down. No similarly concrete criteria were available for the men performing, for example, reconnaissance or artillery-spotting duties – duties that several famous fighter pilots, including Oswald Boelcke and Manfred von Richthofen, considered more important than their own. Another contributory aspect may have been the fighter pilot's growing popularity among the general public. Fighter pilot victories were definitive and occurred on a daily basis, all during a time when millions of men were unsuccessfully bogged down in essentially stagnant trench warfare. Their exploits gave identifiable names and faces to the vast, antlike armies of men confronting one another, and the public could follow their careers much like they could those of sports or movie stars. Fighter pilots also captured the public imagination because they were at the forefront of the age of aviation – something fresh and exciting to most of the world. As a result, the German high command may have subconsciously or even consciously favored the fighter pilot above all other aviator roles.

Another particularly noteworthy aspect of the *Pour le Mérite* aviation awards is the number that went to lower rank officers, i.e., 78 (96.3%) to lieutenants, captains and their naval equivalents, which accounted for nearly half (44.8%) of the war's total *Pour le Mérite* awards (174) to men of such rank. No doubt this was a function of the Air Service's recent establishment, the fact that it was primarily an organization comprised of volunteers, and that flying was essentially a young man's pursuit. But Europe was also growing restless with its ruling classes and the German populace probably found a great deal of satisfaction in the fact that their young sons, many from more humble backgrounds, could be recognized on an equal footing with aristocratic generals.

The number of victories required for a fighter pilot to become eligible for the *Pour le Mérite* increased as the war progressed. We know this not from official documents that spelled out such qualifications, but rather from the timing and events surrounding the awards. The first two airmen to receive the *Pour le Mérite*, Oswald Boelcke and Max Immelmann, were each granted it immediately after their eighth victories (both occurred on 12 January 1916). The next airman recipient, Hans-Joachim Buddecke, may or may not have achieved that total (he had at least seven), but additional consideration may have been given to the fact that the potential for air victories was much lower in his theater of operations (Turkey) than it was for Boelcke and Immelmann (Western Front). After that, however, eight appears to have been the standard applied to the next ten recipients. Today, particularly in light of the totals eventually compiled by many of the war's later fighter pilots, eight downed planes no longer seems like much of a feat; but in 1916, nothing like it had ever been done before. In the first months of the war, aircraft on both sides were unarmed and were only occasionally brought down by antiaircraft fire. As two-seaters began to carry a single machine gun, a few air-to-air victories did occur though they were exceptionally rare. Only with the advent of the armed single-seat fighter plane, which first gained lethal effectiveness in the form of the Fokker *Eindecker* of July 1915, did a flier's scoring run really become possible. By the time of their awards in January 1916, Boelcke and Immelmann had performed in spectacular fashion, keeping up a pace of just over one victory every three weeks. Buddecke had drawn near with five confirmed victories, but the next closest German airmen had three or less. In fact, no other pilot (with the possible exception of Buddecke) was able to equal Boelcke's and Immelmann's eight count until Kurt Wintgens did so in June 1916; and by that point, Immelmann had 15 and Boelcke 19.

There are several indications that the standard was raised on or around 1 November 1916. First, four men achieved their eighth confirmed success that month but did not get the award: Stefan Kirmaier (1 November), Hans Schilling (3 November), Manfred von Richthofen (9 November) and Hans von Keudell (16 November).[3] In fact, Kirmaier and Richthofen each got their eleventh, and Keudell his tenth, before the end of the month. Second, we have the case of Hans Berr. His 4 December award following his tenth victory appears to offer a contradiction. Yet closer investigation reveals that he claimed a balloon on 26 October as his eighth victim and two aircraft on 1 and 2 November as his ninth and tenth. The balloon claim initially went unrecognized, so his ninth and tenth chronological victories were entered in the record as his eighth and ninth. A short time later the balloon claim was allowed, so his chronological eighth was entered as his tenth. Yet someone apparently noticed that he had indeed qualified for the *Pour le Mérite* under the old standard by having attained eight successes prior to 1 November and he was consequently given the decoration on 4 December. Last, we have Manfred von Richthofen's award on 12 January 1917 when he had a total of 16 victories. By that date, seven airmen who had achieved eight or more victories after 1 November had not received the decoration.[4] Therefore, several authors have concluded that the *Pour le Mérite's* qualifying total had been doubled to 16 before Richthofen's award. Yet the new bar might just as easily have been 15. If we return to the pilots who were granted the order upon their eighth victory, we see that it at first came to them on or within a few days of that achievement. Three of the final four, however, had to wait anywhere from 19 to 45 days before they received their decorations.[5] Richthofen brought his 15th victim down on 27 December 1916, so a delay of 16 days until his *Pour le Mérite* came would not have been unusual. The same is true for the airmen who followed Richthofen: (i) Werner Voss – his 15th came down on 11 March 1917 and his *Pour le Mérite* was granted 28 days later on 8 April. (ii) Fritz Otto Bernert – 15th downed on 7 April, award on 23 April (16 days later). (iii) Karl-Emil Schaefer – 15th on 11 April, award on 26 April (11 days). (iv) Kurt Wolff – 15th on 14 April, award on 4 May (20 days). Perhaps it was considered appropriate that only those men who could equal the revered Max Immelmann's final total would qualify for future recognition. At any rate, it seems clear that a higher standard – 15 or 16 victories – had been established by 1 November 1916.

Eventually, the bar was raised even higher to 20. Again, we have no official record to explain why or precisely when. The airmen themselves referred to this hurdle in their writings from mid-1917 forward, and the overall data indeed supports its existence. The fact that some pilots had 30 or more victories before they received their award has led some scholars to speculate that the *Pour le Mérite* qualification level was increased even further to 25 or even 30 in 1918; but as Neal O'Connor pointed out: "The idea that it took at least 30 victories for a fighter pilot to gain the *Pour le Mérite* late in the war is not supported by at least two facts. First, there were 12 of them who received the order in the last half of 1918 with scores below 30 at the time of the award. One approved as late as November 1, 1918 went to a man with 'only' 27 victories. Second, at least 16 fighter pilots had been nominated for the award and were waiting for it to be approved when the war ended. All but three had official scores below 30 when the Armistice and the Kaiser's abdication ended the matter."[6] The high totals that many pilots had amassed by the time of their award appears to have been more a function of the approval process delays experienced during the war's closing months and the rapidity of scoring that occurred in the meantime.

As early as October 1916, Oswald Boelcke (who had been totally surprised by his own award) stated how some men were looking to win the decoration as a goal unto itself because of all the publicity surrounding its airmen recipients: "It is really unfortunate that the public only knows something about us combat fliers. Now all the young men naturally want to become fighter pilots in order to win the *Pour le Mérite* and make a name for themselves."[7] There is no question that most airmen viewed it as the highest form of recognition, and the way its winners were feted at home and in the press fully supported that notion. Future *Pour le Mérite* holder Heinrich Kroll remarked on 26 February 1918: "Dangerous for the fliers are the periods around the 12th and 20th victories. In the first case the *Hohenzollern Haus Orden* is awarded and the *Pour le Mérite* in the second case. Fighter pilots try very hard to get the required number when it seems that they are almost there and sometimes tend to be careless and get themselves shot down!"[8] Though airmen sometimes referred to the coveted decoration with somewhat irreverent nicknames like the "Blue Max," "Blue Star" and "Blue Bird," what they had to undergo to earn it was deadly serious.[9] In addition to the obvious dangers inherent in war, they went up in "crates", Zeppelins and balloons whose structural foibles and anomalies were just as likely to kill them as the enemy. But they assumed those added risks because they wanted to fight for their country, their families, their friends and comrades, their honor, their own lives – and in at least a few instances, the *Orden Pour le Mérite*.

The series that follows will explore the story of each member of the exclusive *Pour le Mérite* aviation club as well as those known to have been nominated for admittance. Though much has been written about these men already, that information is often scattered among a wide variety of sources of varying age, availability and reliability. The goal of this series is to consolidate much of that knowledge in one place for convenient reference along with updated information. Whenever possible, new material and rarely seen photographs will be provided as well. Each aviator's section will begin with a description of his background and career, followed by a detailed account of the aircraft he flew – including color renditions of those aircraft – and a summary of the key event dates, units, awards and victories of his military service record. The airmen will be presented in the order in which they received (or were nominated for) the *Pour le Mérite*. This is being done in order to keep their stories and accomplishments in context with one another as well as with the war's chronology of events.

Endnotes:
[1] Prussia's Golden Military Merit Cross became the equivalent decoration for non-commissioned officers and lower ranks when it was instituted by Wilhelm I on 27 February 1864.
[2] *Aviation Awards of Imperial Germany* 2, p.58. In addition, there were 122 awards of the *Pour le Mérite* with Oakleaves.
[3] Kirmaier, Schilling and Keudell never qualified for the *Pour le Mérite* because they were killed after having attained 11, 8 and 12 victories, respectively.
[4] They were Stefan Kirmaier (11), Hans von Keudell (10), Hartmut Baldamus (9), Erwin Böhme (9), Hans Karl Müller (9), Hans Schilling (8) and Hermann Pfeifer (8).
[5] Rudolf Berthold's eighth fell on 22 September and he was awarded the *Pour le Mérite* on 12 October (20 days later); Albert Dossenbach – eighth on 27 September, award on 11 November (45 days later); Gustav Leffers – eighth on 17 October, award on 5 November (19 days later). The fourth man was Hans Berr whose 39-day period between his eighth (26 October) and the award (4 December) was, as already mentioned, at least partially due to a delayed confirmation of his eighth.
[6] *Aviation Awards of Imperial Germany* 2, p.65.
[7] *Die Woche* 46, p.1606.
[8] *Cross & Cockade* 14:2, p.181. The other medal Kroll referred to was the Royal Hohenzollern House Order, Knight's Cross with Swords that normally preceded a *Pour le Mérite* award.
[9] Even the enemy used at least one sobriquet for the high award, as when one British officer called it the "Boelcke Collar."

Oswald Boelcke

Above: This photograph of Oswald Boelcke was taken right after he was awarded the *Orden Pour le Mérite*.

Boelcke – The Man
Youth

Oswald Boelcke, born on 19 May 1891 in Giebichenstein (near Halle), was the fourth of six children. The Bölcke family moved to Dessau when he was four years old and it was there that Oswald spent his youth.[1] When one writer interviewed Professor Bölcke shortly after Oswald's death, the subject of his son's propensities as a boy came up. He said that his son was "just like any other boy, no better, no worse." He was an average student who enjoyed the sciences and mathematics but was not fond of the classical languages (i.e., Greek, Latin).[2] Where he clearly stood out the most, however, according to both his father and his former headmaster, was in athletic pursuits of almost any kind: gymnastics, ice skating, swimming, diving, tennis, rowing, football and track and field. "He was a strong character who found it absolutely necessary to gain full occupation for his physical strength."[3] Even as a young boy, the skill and daring exhibited in his performances and competitions made a memorable impression on those watching. Young Oswald also took to mountaineering, a pastime at which his father was quite practiced. Timidity and doubts "were foreign to his nature; in fact, the more difficult and dangerous an enterprise was, the more it attracted him."[4]

Not all athletic pursuits came easily to young Oswald, however. He had long wanted to ride a horse and his first opportunity came as a young teen during a visit to his uncle's stables at Freyburg. He was alloted a tame animal and as Prof. Bölcke recalled: "Oswald, who had never mounted the back of a horse, cheekily swung himself into the saddle and proudly trotted away from there." Oswald and the horse disappeared until the evening hours when "the horse trotted quite happily into the yard again and brought the rider into the stable." It turned out that Oswald was unable to control the animal

Above: This portrait of Oswald Boelcke and some of his family was taken at Julius Müller's studio in Dessau in late May 1916 while Boelcke was home on leave. From left to right: Max, Jr., Oswald, mother Mathilde, father Max.

Above: Oswald Boelcke when he was 2 years (left) and 18 years of age (right).

and that it took him on a scenic tour around the outskirts of city until it returned of its own accord. A chagrined Oswald nevertheless remained proud of his first trip in the saddle.[5]

Though mostly obedient and respectful to those in authority, Boelcke still had a wilful streak that compelled him to pursue and push for his goals, no matter the consequences. He displayed this trait early on when the Stillinge Swimming Association organized a swimming and diving meet in Dessau. Oswald was denied participation because a ban existed on high school students taking part in such athletic competitions, so he competed under an assumed name and ended up winning several first prizes.[6] How he first entered the military is another case in point. Without consulting anyone, he wrote a letter to the Kaiser asking him for a nomination to the cadet corps. Boelcke's parents only found this out after they had received a response from the commander of the cadet corps stating that the Kaiser had granted their son's request and asking them to provide the necessary paperwork.[7]

These passages convey many of the key characteristics that manifested themselves in, and thereby shaped, Boelcke's career as a pilot. Clearly, his natural athleticism, impressive coordination and lack of fear of heights later contributed to his extraordinary flying skills. Boelcke was also a "risk taker" who enjoyed new challenges, the sensation of speed and pushing up against physical bounds; yet he relied on both his natural skills and preparation to mold the odds more in his favor. Willy Aschenborn, one of Boelcke's observers at *FFA* 62, related that if Boelcke ever made an imperfect landing after a mission, he would take them both around again and practice his landings until he achieved "a clean touchdown that would not have broken an egg."

Above: Oswald Boelcke as a *Fahnenjunker* (officer candidate) in *Telegraphen-Bataillon* Nr.3.

Aschenborn also stated that Boelcke fervently believed in a strong work ethic that "meant proving oneself through one's actions."[8] Boelcke's father and headmaster characterized him as a man of action too, a trait that led to his being a born leader. His extremely gifted natural abilities, combined with his drive to meet new challenges and get the job done, undoubtedly provided the foundation for the accomplished, pioneering combat pilot that he became.

Early Military Career

As we already saw, Oswald Boelcke decided that he wanted to enter military service as an officer and took the matter up with the Kaiser himself. He was formally accepted into the army as a *Fahnenjunker* (officer candidate) on 15 March 1911, a few months shy of his 20th birthday. Because of his interest in the sciences, he chose to serve with a wireless group and was sent for training with *Telegraphen-Bataillon* Nr.3 at Coblence. His letters home offered various

Above: *Lt.* Boelcke (second from right) and the other officers of *Telegraphen-Bataillon* Nr.3.

details of this training period but indicated that he thrived most on the physical training and riding horses. In September, Boelcke was sent to the region around Strasburg for his first military maneuvers, but found to his dismay that he had little to do of any importance thoughout them. He nonetheless found some solace in a chance encounter: "I gained one very striking impression during my first few days in Strasburg, as the airships and aeroplanes manoeuvering in the neighbourhood often flew over the town. Monoplanes and biplanes flew close to the town tower, which I climbed to get a view of them. Flying is a fine game."[9]

Boelcke attended the cavalry section of the *Kriegsschule* (War Academy) in Metz in October 1911 to receive advanced training. He told his parents about the physical side (exercising, drills, riding, shooting and even lance training) but made little mention of the academics except to report on 13 December that he had done sufficiently well to have been excused from all future evening classes. Aviation continued to draw his attention as when he wrote on 18 April 1912: "But generally I go out to the big parade-ground at Frescaty, where there are several monoplanes and biplanes flying every evening. One monoplane makes particularly fine flights (glides, etc.). I never get tired of watching and always stare at them with eyes of longing. It must be a wonderful sport – more beautiful even than riding!"[10]

Following Boelcke's correspondence as his military training advanced provides numerous insights into the man's evolution. His leadership talents and affinity for instruction particularly manifested themselves, as in the following excerpts: "...I got all 'goods' and 'very goods' in my viva voce. Unfortunately, parts of my written exams were only 'fair,' so that the final verdict was only a 'good.' But that does not matter, because I came off best of the three ensigns here, which means that I am now the senior in the battalion. Also, as my commander told me today, I got a 9 (excellent) for 'leadership.'" (8 July 1912); "I drilled my telegraph recruits for the first time today. It is great fun for me to turn these civilians into decent soldiers...As soon as I see signs of good will I am satisfied – inwardly at least – even though I have to curse the clumsy beggars a bit." (21 October 1912); "My recruits are making capital progress...The chief thing, it seems to me, is to inculcate a liking and love for the service, and such

Above: Adolphe Pégoud was a pioneer pilot and instructor before the war who specialized in stunt-flying. He inspired Boelcke during one of his flying displays at Frankfurt in 1913. France's first ace in the Great War, Pégoud was later killed in combat by one of his former German students on 31 August 1915.

entertainments after the arduous labour of their drill are a great help in that direction. You thus see that I get much pleasure out of my recruit school." (1 November 1912).[11]

His fascination with aviation continued to grow, as when he reported on 21 November 1913: "Last Saturday I went to Frankfurt to see Pégoud, the Frenchman, fly. You can hardly believe what that fellow can do – somersaults, vertical dives, turns over the vertical, upside down flying, etc. – and all with such confidence and assurance that you cannot for a moment feel he will crash. The man made a very great impression on me."[12]

What Boelcke neglected to tell his parents was that he had gone up for his first plane ride in June 1913 while at Metz. According to his friend, *Lt.* Baltzer: "When we were sent to Metz in June, 1913, on a three days' course at the wireless station there and took the opportunity to pay a visit to the aerodrome at Frescaty, we were taken up for our first flight in an aeroplane and were both enraptured with it. Afterwards, we had plenty of opportunities to watch the flying at Griesheim; in consequence of the lack of observers we had the chance of making many short and long flights. We both enjoyed them immensely, but decided to say nothing about them in our letters home in order to avoid causing unnecessary anxiety to our parents. We saw much of the flying officers..."[13] One of them was *Lt.* Otto Parschau, who would play an even more important role in Boelcke's life during the war.

With temptation so near on a daily basis, and with his older brother Wilhelm already having become an observer in the fledgling air service, Boelcke was induced to request a transfer to flight training in April 1914.

Airman

Boelcke was accepted as a pilot trainee in late May and arrived at Halberstadt's flight school on 2 June 1914 – one year after his first trip in an airplane. His record demonstrates how fast a learner he was. Training in "Bristol-*Taube*" monoplanes, Boelcke was occasionally handed the controls by his instructor within two weeks of his arrival. His first solo flight followed on 2 July and after only three more he passed his first pilot's examination on 13 July.[14] He conquered the second Pilot's Exam on 31 July – the day war was declared – and was then sent to *Flieger-Ersatz-Abteilung* 3 near Darmstadt pending further orders. Boelcke languished there, thoroughly annoyed, for almost a month before being ordered to *Etappen-Flugzeug-Park* 4 at Trier to await further disposition to the Front. He had completed his final Pilots' Exam on 15 August and wanted to join his brother Wilhelm's unit, *FFA* 13. He was given a perfect opening when he learned that *FFA* 13 was in need of two replacements. When he asked permission to report as one of them, the deputy commander of the Trier base informed him that only the CO – who was away at the time – could grant such permission. This is where Boelcke's wilful streak came into play. He had an opportunity to gain what he wanted and was not about to let the CO's inconvenient absence stand in the way. Boelcke knew that part of the Trier group was being transferred to another *Flugpark* at Sedan, so he asked if he could assist by flying a plane there. This time the deputy CO granted his request, not knowing that Boelcke planned to have a "forced landing" at *FFA* 13's airfield along the way. Once there, he would offer his services as a replacement; if rebuffed, he would continue on to Sedan with no one the wiser. Fortunately for Boelcke, *FFA* 13's head man, *Hptm.* Hans Streccius, jumped at the offer and "took the responsibillity for my non-arrival at Sedan."[15] The next day, 1 September 1914, Boelcke went up on his first mission against the enemy with brother Wilhelm as his observer: "We cruised over the enemy's positions at a height of two thousand eight hundred metres for about an hour and a half, until Wilhelm had spied out everything...Wilhelm's report enabled our artillery to

Left: The unarmed Fokker M.8 monoplane that the military designated type A.I.

place their first rounds so accurately that the French artillery were forced to abandon their positions at once."[16] For the next six months, he and Wilhelm flew almost exclusively together while *FFA* 13 was shunted about from La Ferté-sur-Chiers to Chatel-Chéhéry, Sainte-Menehould, Buzancy and Pontfaverger-Moronvilliers. Boelcke's acquaintance from Griesheim, *Lt.* Otto Parschau, flew to *FFA* 13's Pontfaverger airfield in a Fokker A.II/M.5L monoplane on 11 November 1914.

This unarmed reconnaissance aircraft, a predecessor of the E.I fighter, was relatively new to the conflict and was significantly smaller and faster than anything Boelcke had flown before. Its appeal was therefore irresistible and Boelcke went to the *Armee-Flug-Park* at Rethel to obtain one on 23 November; but he was turned away because the only one there had already been reserved for another officer. In keeping with his nature, Boelcke persevered and was able to pick up a Fokker A.I/M.8 at Rethel on 8 December. He called it his "big Christmas present, about which I am as delighted as a child."[17] He was so excited about the plane that he spent much of the next day giving rides to Wilhelm and several other officers (the plane accommodated two occupants, sitting close in tandem). Apparently, Boelcke alternated between flying his LVG biplane and Fokker monoplane from this point forward, though he offered few details in this regard.

By 4 January 1915, Wilhelm had made 61 flights into enemy territory and Oswald, despite being the last of *FFA* 13's airmen to join the unit, had made 42. The next closest were "Sander twenty-seven, Karstedt twenty-two and Beckers twenty."[18] Due to their outstanding efforts, both classes of the Iron Cross were awarded to the industrious brothers, with Oswald's coming on 12 October 1914 (2nd Class) and 27 January 1915 (1st Class).[19] Oswald was also decorated with his native Anhalt's Friedrich Cross, 2nd Class on 31 January.

Hptm. Streccius, *FFA* 13's CO, was bumped up to a staff officer position at the end of 1914. In early 1915, his replacement decided to break up the Boelcke brothers' partnership, but would not provide any reason why when asked. Consequently, as Oswald put it: "...we went on strike. We reported the matter to H.Q. and asked for a transfer to another section. His Excellency must have said a few things to our Captain, because all of a sudden he caved in and now leaves us in peace."[20] It was the calm before the storm, however, because Wilhelm was suddenly transferred without warning to a *Flieger-Ersatz-Abteilung* in Posen on 4 April 1915. His headstrong actions having backfired, Oswald was both devastated and angry. He wrote home the same day: "For the time being, the doctor was kind enough to discover 'faint sounds' in my bronchial tubes and send me to a convalescent home for three weeks."[21] Whether this was a manufactured illness in collusion with the doctor or a real one (Boelcke did have a history of bronchial complaints) is unclear. In any event, he reported to Château-Porcien two days later, "...only too glad to turn my back on Pontfaverger and the chief of the 13th

Above: *Lt.* Otto Parschau (left) and Boelcke. Parschau introduced Boelcke to Fokker's monoplanes.

section."[22] What Boelcke did not know is that his superiors had taken an interest in the matter too. *General* Kurt von Pritzelwitz, commander of the *VI. Armee-Korps* to which *FFA* 13 was attached, told the hospital's chief physician to keep him there because he did not want to lose both Wilhelm and Oswald. When Boelcke became aware of this, he decided it was of no further benefit to remain at the hospital and was granted permission to return to his unit. His stay was brief though because he learned on 25 April that he was to go to a new *Abteilung* (*FFA* 62) being assembled outside Döberitz under the command of veteran airman *Hptm.* Hermann Kastner. Fortune had smiled on Oswald Boelcke, after all.

Boelcke arrived at Döberitz in May and quickly struck up a friendship with *Lt.* Willy Aschenborn, who like Boelcke, was already an experienced veteran. They decided to team up, subject to a trial flight together from Döberitz to Boelcke's parents' house in Ziebigk bei Dessau. This flight took place in an old LVG B.I that left a poor impression on them. Aschenborn explained that they felt the B.I (derisively referred to as the "bathtub" or "B-minor") was too slow for current war conditions, so they sought out another type. They became aware of a smaller, faster B.II being overhauled at the

Right: Willy Aschenborn, Oswald Boelcke's observer in May–June 1915, stated the Boelcke focused heavily on machine guns and their operation after the arrival of armed LVG C.I biplanes and Fokker E.I monoplanes at *FFA* 62. This photo captures Boelcke as a keen observer during one of the machine gun training sessions held there. From left to right: *Lt.* Heinz Hellmut von Wühlisch, Boelcke, *Lt.* Porr, *Lt.* Ehrhardt von Teubern and Max Immelmann. *Hptm.* Ritter is manning the gun.

nearby factory but *Idflieg* (Inspectorate of Flying Troops) repeatedly denied their request for it. Then "through our tenacious efforts, combined with a little impudence," they nevertheless succeeded in commandeering it and exchanged it for their old B.I on the eve of their departure to the Front. "Happy and content, we then went to the Front with this best of machines compared to all others."[23]

Accompanying them was *Fähnrich* Max Immelmann, who had been transferred out of *FFA* 10 in the Champagne region after only 13 days of service. Aschenborn recalled: "A strange twist of fate also led to then *Fähnrich* (officer candidate) Immelmann being sent back to the homeland to the same *Abteilung* from a field in the Champagne region with the note: 'Completely unsuitable as an airplane pilot at the Front!' This was because of too many crash landings."[24] Prof. Werner offered a similar assessment: "Although accepted for the air service at the beginning of the war, he did not pass his third set of tests until March 26th, 1915, after which he served in the Champagne, where he won the reputation of being a specialist in the art of crashing his machine on landing."[25] It would only be a matter of months, however, before Immelmann garnered a much different reputation.

Boelcke was in familiar territory when *FFA* 62 arrived at Pontfaverger-Montvilliers on 15 May, but after only a few days the unit moved on by rail to Douai, where it would remain for over a year. Boelcke flew with Aschenborn on most of his missions until mid-June's arrival of the first German operational aircraft specifically designed to carry a machine gun: the LVG C.I. Boelcke had demonstrated his aggressive tendencies only a few weeks earlier by specially modifying a previously defenseless LVG B.II with a captured French machine gun. Because of this, *FFA* 62's first C.I was turned over to Boelcke, who consequently replaced Aschenborn with *Lt.* Heinz Hellmut von Wühlisch, a man already familiar with machine gunnery. Though the men took to referring to the C.I as a "*Kampfflugzeug*" ("combat plane"), they saw the real thing on 23 June when Anthony Fokker and *Lt.* Otto Parschau demonstrated two Fokker fighters at Douai in front of Rupprecht, Crown Prince of Bavaria, and *FFAs* 62 and 20.

The impact on Boelcke was immediate and irrevocable. Boelcke's flight log noted that his first trial flight in an E.I occurred the next day on 24 June. Aschenborn related: "...from then on his entire being and flying ambitions were concentrated on this machine. His leisure hours were spent on machine gun firing practice and he could not strip and reassemble the gun often enough in order to learn every last detail about it."[26]

While familiarizing himself with the small fighter, Boelcke continued flying LVG C.I 162/15 in combat and on 4 July, he and Wühlisch at last succeeded in shooting down an enemy plane: "On

Above: Boelcke (left) and his observer/machine-gunner, *Lt.* Heinz Hellmut von Wühlisch, pose atop the wreckage of their first victory, brought down on 4 July 1916.

Sunday I succeeded for the first time in carrying a fight through to complete victory. I had orders to protect Lieut. Porr, who was spotting for the artillery, against enemy aircraft. I had hardly started on my way to the front before we saw a French Parasol monoplane over Liétard that was approaching us from a greater height. As the lower machine is at a disadvantage, we got out of his way; he did not see us, but flew onward and downward. We were delighted to see him, because the French machines have seldom crossed our lines lately and an opponent cannot get away in a glide if he is over our territory.

As soon as he was past us, we started to chase him but took quite half an hour before we came up with him over Valenciennes. It would seem that he was very late in sighting us. We started to engage him near Valenciennes, where I tried to cut him off. Luckily we were the speedier, so that he was unable to get away from us by turns. As soon as we got close enough, Wühlisch began to pepper him with the machine gun. He defended himself as well as he could, but we remained the aggressors and kept him on the defensive; we were higher and faster, while he was lower and slower, so that he could not possibly escape us. He tried to increase the distance between the two machines by all sorts of manoeuvres, but did not succeed – I sat on his neck all the time. It was a glorious business. I hung on close to him, so that Wühlisch could shoot steadily from short range. We could see all the details of his machine quite clearly; we could almost spot every wire on it. The average distance was about one hundred metres, but sometimes I got up to within thirty and forty metres of him, because the great speed at which aeroplanes fly affords no prospects of success except from a very close range.

The whole fight lasted from twenty to twenty-five minutes; in its course we came close to Marchiennes. There were brief intervals in our fire, occasioned by the enemy's turn, jams and reloading of the machine gun; these I utilised to come up with the Frenchman and get close to him. Our superiority became more and more evident; at last I gained the impression that the enemy had stopped defending himself and nearly given up hope of escape. Shortly before the machine crashed the observer made a typical gesture with his hand, as if to say: 'Let us alone; we are beaten and will surrender.' But who can trust an aerial opponent in such cases?

Thereupon he went into a glide – I followed closely behind. My observer fired another thirty to forty rounds, and then the machine suddenly vanished. I went into a steep glide so as not to lose close contact with him, and then all of a sudden Wühlisch shouted: 'he's falling, he's falling!' and whacked my shoulders with joy. I did not quite trust that Frenchman, because those monoplanes can go into a steep dive that looks very like a fall, and so stared round in astonishment, but could see nothing more. I went down in a glide, and meanwhile Wühlisch told me that the other machine suddenly heeled over and fell vertically into the wood below us.

We dropped down to one hundred metres and scoured the wood for the fallen machine, but could discover no signs of it. Then we decided to land on a meadow close to the wood and look for it... We climbed out to go and see. On the way we met Captain Bieler, whom I knew from Pontfaverger times; he took us in his car and told us that everyone in the district had followed the fight from below. They were all very excited...The full weight of the machine struck a tree; it was smashed to bits, while the inmates, a hussar lieutenant named Tétu and a certain Comte Beauvicourt, were naturally dead – strangely enough the latter was the owner of the wood into which he had crashed...the pilot had seven and the observer five bullet wounds."[27]

Willy Aschenborn had this to say about Boelcke's first victory: "To all our amazement, he revealed a completely undreamt-of flying skill in this, his first fully successful air combat. He moved in on the enemy, continually pressed him down (often so close that one feared a collision at any moment) from 2500 to 1000 meters, yet always stayed mindful of keeping him within the field of fire of his observer's machine gun. This method was entirely new and thereby laid the groundwork for his later air battles and successes. It did so too for fighter aviation as a whole, because what he instinctively applied as a tactic and method for carrying out the battle during this chance engagement became its foundation and ruling law."[28]

Fighter Pilot
Boelcke never looked back. Three days later, despite his victory in the LVG C.I, he switched over to flying his Fokker E.I almost exclusively: "I have been flying my Fokker single-seater since last Wednesday. I shall seldom fly biplanes now. I am sorry to part company with Wühlisch – we worked splendidly together. On the other hand I am highly delighted, because I believe in the saying that 'the strong man is mightiest alone.' I have attained my ideal with this single-seater; now I can be pilot, observer and fighter all in one."[29] Oswald Boelcke, supremely confident in his own abilities, had made up his mind to become one of the world's first fighter pilots.

Boelcke wrote on 16 July that he was particularly enjoying the independence afforded him by the E.I monoplane. The French, however, were not cooperating in his new venture: "As soon as I appear on the scene, they bolt as quick as they can. As I cannot catch any of them here, I go to look for them on their side of the lines where they think they can spot for their artillery in safety. I have to prowl about stealthily and invisibly, using every trick and wile I can manage. In this fashion I have succeeded in shooting at four of them, but as they always make a dive for home at once, I could not get any of them because I cannot chase them too far behind the enemy's lines without exposing myself to their artillery...One must not wait till they come across, but seek them out and hunt them down."[30]

The English decided to try to remove this new threat when they mounted two bombing raids on FFA 62's aerodrome on 1 August. They probably were unaware, however, that they would have to contend with two of the new Eindecker fighters. Just a few days earlier, Leutnant Max Immelmann (who had achieved that rank as of 14 July) had asked Boelcke to tutor him in flying Fokker's machine. So during the second bombing run, while Boelcke chased after a "French monoplane," Immelmann took off after four BE.2s from RFC No.2 Squadron and shot one of them down.[31] Boelcke probably would have gotten his quarry too if not for a last minute gun jam. His mixed emotions at Immelmann having gained FFA 62's first Eindecker victory are evident in his 11 August letter home: "Immelmann was extraordinarily lucky concerning the whole business. Three days earlier I had trained him for the first time on a Fokker, i.e., I flew with him and let him take over the controls. The day before was the first time he had flown solo and he was only able to land with considerable difficulty. He had never flown nor fired his machine gun against the enemy [in a Fokker] – and then he had the luck to catch a defenseless biplane over our aerodrome, because the Englishman had left his observer at home to save weight for his bombs. All the same Immelmann did his job beautifully and I congratulate him sincerely on his success. But I really am annoyed at my own bad luck; it was the first time for four weeks that I got an opponent bang in front of my gun, and then it must go and jam!"[32]

Boelcke caught up with Immelmann on 19 August. He forced three enemy planes down that day behind their own lines but was unsure if he had seriously damaged any of them. He noted that the first, however, had suddenly lost power and disappeared below. It was later observed by German gunners to have force-landed among English artillery positions, so this likely is the victory that German authorities subsequently attributed to Boelcke. If so, then his first victory in an Eindecker probably was the RFC No.2 Squadron machine whose crew

Victories Scored by Boelcke and Immelmann

Date	Boelcke	Immelmann
15 Jul 1915	Vic 1	
1 Aug 1915		Vic 1
19 Aug 1915	Vic 2	
10 Sep 1915	Vic 3	Vic 2
21 Sep 1915		Vic 3
24 Sep 1915	Vic 4	
10 Oct 1915		Vic 4
16 Oct 1915	Vic 5	
26 Oct 1915		Vic 5
30 Oct 1915	Vic 6	
7 Nov 1915		Vic 6
15 Dec 1915		Vic 7
5 Jan 1916	Vic 7	
12 Jan 1916	Vic 8	Vic 8
14 Jan 1916	Vic 9	
2 Mar 1916		Vic 9
12 Mar 1916	Vic 10	
13 Mar 1916	Vic 11	Vics 10, 11
19 Mar 1916	Vic 12	
21 Mar 1916	Vic 13	
29 Mar 1916		Vic 12
30 Mar 1916		Vic 13
23 Apr 1916		Vic 14
27 Apr 1916	Vic 14	
1 May 1916	Vic 15	
16 May 1916		Vic 15
18 May 1916	Vic 16	
21 May 1916	Vics 17, 18	

Left: Boelcke (center) sits down to a meal with *FFA* 62 mates *Lt.* Ernst Hess (left) and *Lt.* Max Immelmann (right). *Lt.* Albert Oesterreicher, in flight gear, watches in the background.

– Cpts. J.G Hearson and Barker – reported that they had been forced to land near Arras due to a severed fuel pipe. Though the standards applied later in the war usually did not accept such a forced landing behind friendly lines as an outright victory, the days of aerial warfare claims were still young and German authorities evidently allowed this example early on.

There are numerous written accounts of the victories that Boelcke and Immelmann continued to compile until Immelmann's death on 18 June 1916 so they will not be reviewed again here in any detail.[33] A summary of their victory dates (see p.15), however, is useful in demonstrating the close – though friendly – competition that arose between the two airmen.[34]

Their parallel records seem even more remarkable when one considers that the two men were separated twice during this period. The first time occurred when Boelcke was secretly sent off to *Brieftauben-Abteilung Metz (B.A.M.)*, where he arrived on 21 September 1915.[35] Even Immelmann was not sure where or why Boelcke had gone away. They were reunited again around 12 December 1915 until Boelcke departed on 21 January 1916 to serve with a Fokker detachment in support of *Artillerie-Flieger-Abteilung* 203 at Jametz. Despite being at different sections of the Front under different conditions, they still managed to keep pace with one another.

An extraordinary event occurred in Boelcke's

Boelcke's Dicta

1. Seek an advantage before attacking. If possible, keep the sun behind you.
2. Once you've started an attack, always carry it through.
3. Fire only at close range and only when the opponent is properly in your sights.
4. Always keep your eye on your opponent, and don't let yourself be deceived by ruses.
5. Whenever you attack, it's important to go at your opponent from behind.
6. If your opponent attacks you from above, don't try to evade him but fly right at him.
7. When you are over enemy territory, never forget your own line of retreat.
8. For the *Staffel*: attack on principle in a group of four or six; but when the fight breaks down into individual combats, several shouldn't go after a single opponent.

Above: In early July 1916, Chief of Field Aviation Hermann Thomsen met with Oswald Boelcke at German Supreme Headquarters at Charleville. "At my request he drew up the following summary of the principles that should govern every air fight; briefly composed and simply expressed, they were also to serve as a source of success for the younger scouts. These principles established by Boelcke remained in force until the end of the war." Indeed, they were only slightly revised and employed by fighter pilots until the age of jets and avionics. Because of Boelcke's Dicta (see above) and the fact that he was the first pilot to create and promote fighter team tactics in the air, he is often recognized as the father of fighter aviation.

Above: This is one of many pictures taken of Boelcke's 7th victim. This one shows Boelcke (blurry figure in the dark overcoat at far left) inspecting the remains.

life a little less than a month before his departure to *B.A.M.* that played perfectly into his tendency to take action as well as his excellent swimming abilities. *FFA 62*'s mess was situated on a canal in which the local inhabitants often fished, facing a jetty where various small boats unloaded their cargo. On 28 August 1915, Boelcke and *Lt.* Ehrhardt von Teubern were standing at the building's front door after lunch when they saw a boy climb a railing with his fishing gear and suddenly tumble into the water. Boelcke, the "man of action," immediately dove in after him. After surfacing from what proved to be an unsuccessful first attempt, Boelcke spotted a small number of bubbles nearby. He swam over to them, dove again and this time managed to grab the drowning boy underwater. He rose up with the lad in tow and shouted to Teubern and another soldier to get into one of the boats moored nearby and push out to him. He dragged the boy to it, Teubern pulled him in and Boelcke joined them in safety. Meanwhile, the youngster's mother had arrived on scene and she thanked Boelcke profusely with a torrent of words. "The rest of the civilians also gave me an ovation. I must have been a fine sight, because I was in full uniform when I hopped in and stood there like a dripping poodle."[36] Boelcke's CO, *Hptm.* Hermann Kastner, recommended him for the Prussian Life Saving Medal but the boy's parents wanted to do one better: "The folks told me they would gladly get the French Legion of Honor for me if they could. That would be such fun, wouldn't it?"[37] As a result of the rescue, Boelcke was indeed awarded Prussia's Life Saving Medal on 30 November 1915, though he did not actually receive it until 12 December 1915 after his return to *FFA 62*. The entire incident so pleased Boelcke that the medal's ribbon was one of only two that he displayed on his tunic.

Boelcke downed victims four through six while with *B.A.M.* His first mention in the *Heeresbericht* (the official military communiqués) appeared on 26 September following his fourth: "*Leutnant* Boelcke, who was ascending on a test flight, caused a Voisin

Above: A typical newspaper publication trumpeting the award of the *Orden Pour le Mérite* to Boelcke and Immelmann.

airplane to crash south of Metz." This succinct passage thrust Boelcke's exploits before the eyes of the German nation. Following his sixth victory on 30 October, Boelcke received word via a 1 November telegram that he was to be awarded the Royal Hohenzollern House Order, Knight's Cross with Swords (the award document was actually executed on 3 November 1915).[38] This was a singular honor at the time and Boelcke was the first airman to be so decorated. It also established a benchmark of six victories as the requirement for an airman to win the Hohenzollern Order – a requirement that would last for a year until 1 November 1916 when it was raised to eight. Boelcke's native Anhalt decided to follow suit and gave him its House Order of Albert the Bear, Knight's Cross 2nd Class with Swords on 8 November. That evening, after a banquet held in his honor in Charleville, *Feldflugchef* (Chief of Field Aviation) *Major* Hermann Thomsen pinned both awards on Boelcke himself.

As the French offensive in the Champagne came to a close, Boelcke was returned to *FFA 62* in Douai on or around 11 December, where he was greeted

Above: Boelcke's *Ordenskissen* that was used to display all but two of his awards at his funeral ceremonies. Starting at the top, we see his *Pour le Mérite*. The next row down, from left to right: Pilot's Badge; Iron Cross, 2nd Class; Royal Hohenzollern House Order, Knight's Cross with Swords; Life Saving Medal; House Order of Albert the Bear, Knight's Cross 1st Class with Swords; House Order of Albert the Bear, Knight's Cross 2nd Class with Swords; Friedrich Cross, 2nd Class; Military Merit Order, 4th Class with Swords; Turkish Pilot's Badge. The Military Merit Order, Knight and Iron Cross, 1st Class are next below. The bottom row, left to right: Bravery Order, 4th Class, 2nd Degree; War Medal ("Gallipoli Star"); Imtiaz Medal in Silver. Missing were the Saxe-Ernestine House Order, Knight 1st Class with Swords and the Order of the Iron Crown, 3rd Class with War Decoration. The former, awarded on 31 July 1916, is in a family member's possession so we know Boelcke received it. Neither it nor the medals awarded after it were attached to Boelcke's *Grossordenschnalle* (the medals bar visible at upper center) so it may simply have been overlooked. Evidently, the Order of the Iron Crown was awarded too late (25 October 1916) to have been included.

by *Hptm.* Hermann Kastner with Prussia's Life Saving Medal the next day. Another award followed on 24 December 1915: the *Ehrenbecher*, a silver goblet that from then on would be awarded to every army airman upon his first victory. Two of the earliest examples were presented to Boelcke and Immelmann during *FFA* 62's Christmas celebrations. By that point, Boelcke had upgraded his *Eindecker* mount to a Fokker E.IV, which carried two machine guns instead of one. It was in this machine, E.IV 123/15, that he achieved his seventh victory on 5 January 1916.

Both Boecke and Immelmann downed their eighth victories on the morning of 12 January 1916. The rapid response was their simultaneous bestowals of the *Orden Pour le Mérite* that evening. Such immediacy indicates that either higher authorities had planned ahead or the Kaiser had acted impulsively, as he was sometimes prone to do. In either event, a level of eight victories was thereby established as qualification for the decoration until it was later doubled to sixteen as of 1 November 1916. According to their own accounts, nobody was more surprised than Boelcke and Immelmann themselves; and the momentousness of their awards cannot be overemphasized. Before this, Prussia's highest award for bravery had been handed out only 71 times within a span of 17½ months: 57 of them to generals, two to admirals, eight to royalty and one to a Chief of General Staff.[39] Only three had gone to lower rank officers. Two were to *Kptlt.* Otto Hersing and *Oblt.z.See* Otto Weddigen, both submarine commanders who had sunk several large warships, and the other recognized *Lt.* Otto von der Linde after he and his small squad of German soldiers had duped the commander of a Belgian fortress, his five officers and 420 soldiers into surrendering to them on 24 August 1914. Like the Hohenzollern House Order preceding it, Boelcke and Immelmann were the first airmen to receive the *Pour le Mérite*. They were also only the second and third *Leutnante* among the entire German military to be so honored. This recognition heightened the German nation's pride and confidence in its fledgling *Fliegertruppe* (Army Air Service) as well as in the mettle of its more common officers. The men were instantly raised to the status of national heroes whose exploits the German media would continue to follow with

Above: A grainy snapshot of Boelcke (right) and Werner Notzke sitting atop one of the canvas tents set up for their aircraft at Sivry.

Above: The remains of Boelcke's 13th victory after it had crashed near Les Fosses Wood. Note the cannon at center foreground.

particular interest; and their accomplishments were even recognized in the newspapers and magazines of their enemies. The world war had brought with it worldwide notoriety.

Boelcke was uncomfortable with that kind of celebrity, however. As early as 16 July 1915 after his first victory, he remarked: "Father asks whether my report may be published in the papers. You know that I do not think much of publicity in the press. Moreover I consider that my victory does not afford the proper style and scope for a paper. The good readers want a more poetic and awesome description, with psychical tension of fear-tortured nerves torn to shreds, followed by exultant glee, clouds that tower like Alps or the blue sky of heaven full of whispering zephyrs, etc. If, however, it would give you great pleasure to see it published, I shall not object. But naturally no names must appear."[40] On another occasion he told his father: "The Berlin Illustration Company will manage quite well without my photo – I beg you not to send them one. I don't like all this publicity – I find quite enough articles in the papers about myself to be sick of it all."[41] Talking about his recent experiences as a *Pour le Mérite* holder, he complained: "Now here comes the drawback of the medal. Everybody is congratulating me, I am invited everywhere, and they all ask me the same questions – if most of the questioners weren't 'big shots', there is nothing I would like better than to print another sheet of questions and answers."[42] He soon understood, however, that he would have to learn to accept his new status, as when he grudgingly relented in providing a photo to *Die Woche* (a weekly publication) but still categorically refused a book request from well-known publisher August Scherl: "I enclose a couple of the new photos. If the 'Woche' is absolutely determined to have one, send it along as far as I am concerned – as a knight of the '*Pour le Mérite*' I can no longer keep myself out of the press. But Herr Scherl had no luck when he made his offer for a book."[43] Acceptance was one thing, but liking it was another as when he self-mockingly penned this note on the back of a postcard that featured his image: "*Findet Ihr mich schön? Ich nicht!*" ("Do you find me nice? I don't!"). The attention lavished on him whenever he went back to Germany was even more disconcerting to him: "...I learnt by experience how conspicuous a young officer with the '*Pour le Mérite*' appears at home – it is worse than having a warrant out against you. They stared at me all the time in the streets, both in Frankfurt and in Wiesbaden... Also the people in the Opera crowded round me in each interval – it was terrible. But the worst was yet to come. When the opera-singer Schramm sang the well-known aria, 'Father, mother, sisters, brothers' he was loudly applauded and encored. At last he reappeared to start his encore. But just imagine – I could hardly believe my ears – the fellow did not sing the proper words but a verse in my honor which they had hastily strung together behind the scenes – it sounds like it... But then you should just have seen the audience going raving mad; they clapped, shouted and tramped their feet. In the next interval I was the target of all opera glasses – then I saved myself from further ovations by speedy flight."[44] The next time he went to his homeland, he tried traveling incognito by hiding his *Pour le Mérite* – which was required to be worn at all times – under his collar (see p.21 below). Tellingly, no photograph exists of Boelcke wearing all his medals (unlike Immelmann).[45] In fact, there is no picture of

Above: This rare photograph captures the wreckage of *Lt.* Werner Notzke's Fokker E.III 211/16 in front of the balloon (being hauled down) that was instrumental in his fatal accident.

him even with a *Grossordenschnalle* (medals bar) or *Feldschnalle* that displayed their ribbons.

Boelcke and Immelmann physically received their *Pour le Mérite* orders on 17 January when Crown Prince Rupprecht of Bavaria personally decorated both knights during a luncheon ceremony at Lille. Then Boelcke again left *FFA* 62 under a shroud of secrecy four days later. He only knew that he was to go to Montmédy to await further orders. Once there, he was informed that he had been promoted to *Oberleutnant* and assigned to *Artillerie-Flieger-Abteilung (AFA)* 203's base at Jametz, where he was to provide protective cover for the unit's important artillery-spotting activites during the Verdun offensive planned for mid-February. It appears, however, that he eventually convinced his superiors that he would be better employed in the more aggressive role of a hunter and interceptor of the enemy's aircraft, because he was granted permission in the spring of 1916 to find a separate base closer to the Front for his Fokker. He personally selected a meadow near Sivry that was only 7½ miles behind the lines and brought along *Lt.* Werner Notzke as his partner. Prof. Werner correctly concluded: "Thus Boelcke became the leader of an independent though diminutive 'group' of scouts which was detached from the section and solely responsible to the staff officer commanding the air forces. The significance of these 'groups', which were first established in the neighbourhood of Verdun, and their connection with the development of scout-flying has already been discussed: they represent the first stations on the road to the organised *Jagdstaffels*."[46] Another important step had been taken in the evolution of the fighter pilot.

Boelcke arrived at Sivry on 11 March 1916 and, wasting no time in getting to work, bagged his tenth victory the next day and his eleventh the day after that. His 12th occurred on 19 March followed by his 13th on 21 March: "There was really no fight with him, just a quick bit of shooting. About 11 a.m. I saw a German biplane fighting a Farman biplane away to the west of Ornes. I naturally charged down on the latter, got on to him from behind and opened fire from close range, about eighty metres away. As I came down diagonally from above, I got to him in a very few seconds. At the very moment that I was pulling my machine up to clear the enemy, I saw him explode – I got a black pillar of smoke in my face. It was a spectacle of ghastly beauty to see the machine break out in flames and then fall like a huge torch. Its remains are on the ground to the east of Les Fosses Wood... By the way, that Farman had a 3.5 cm. cannon on board – that is the second machine armed with a cannon that has fallen into our hands."[47]

Boelcke's partnership with Notzke came to a tragic end on 21 April when the latter, while test-firing his guns from the air near Sivry field, ran into the cable of a tethered balloon that had been raised there for the first time that same morning. Boelcke was noticeably affected by Notzke's loss when he

BOELKE REPORTED KILLED.

Aeroplane Like German Champion's Is Brought Down by Ribiere.

LONDON, June 17.—Captain Boelke, the champion German aviator, who received an autograph letter from the Emperor recently complimenting him on his success in bringing down French aeroplanes, is believed to have been killed in an aerial combat with the French aviator, Roger Ribiere.

A Fokker painted yellow and of the type known to have been piloted by Boelke, who also wore a large yellow muffler, was shot down by Ribiere two days ago between the German and French trenches near Verdun.

Captain Boelke and his colleague, Lieutenant Immelmann, have been mentioned more times in the German official statement than any other aviators in the aerial branch of the Teuton army. Up to May 21 Captain Boelke had accounted for eighteen French aeroplanes. The last hostile machine brought down by him was vanquished in an aerial battle over Dead Man Hill in the region of Verdun.

A month ago the German airman was promoted from the rank of Lieutenant to that of Captain by Emperor William in acknowledgment of his achievements.

Above & Right: These are the two articles in *The New York Times* that initially reported Boelke's death but then printed Victor Chapman's testimony that Boelke was still very much alive.

BOELKE STILL FIGHTING, AMERICAN AIRMEN SAY

Victor Chapman Thinks He Fought Noted German Aviator on Saturday.

Special Cable to THE NEW YORK TIMES.

PARIS, June 20.—According to American airmen there is no truth in the report that Boelke, the noted German aviator, was recently killed in a duel with a French airman. A letter just received here from Victor Chapman, a member of the American squadron, says:

"Last Saturday I had the narrowest escape to date. Coming home late from a reconnoissance alone, I was attacked from behind by a Fokker swooping from a great height. This, I think, was Boelke, as that is his invariable method of attack. A regular hail of bullets all round the machine riddled it. The controls were so damaged that only by holding them with the hand was I able to make a landing. I was lucky to get off with a light scalp wound, insufficient to cause me to leave the front."

Mr. Chapman added that his assailant was flying a black machine which coincides with American accounts of Boelke. In contradiction of a Matin story which described him as wearing yellow headgear and flying a yellow machine, Americans say that Boelke's aeroplane is black with a huge skull painted under each wing. This, they think, is a deliberate attempt to unnerve the opponents upon whom he swoops.

Mr. Chapman was also in a perilous position Friday evening, when he was surrounded by a group of enemies, but Rockwell came to his rescue and the two eluded the Germans without injury.

German air raiders bombarded Bar-le-Duc on Friday and Saturday. On Friday the Americans would in ordinary circumstances have returned before the raid, which occurred about dusk, but all prolonged their work in the hope of accomplishing something to mark the day, which was the anniversary of the great Artois battle last year, when the first regiment of the Foreign Legion suffered severely and four Americans, Weeks, Kelly, Fike, and Hall, were killed.

broke the news to his parents, probably because he had seldom actually experienced the death of a close comrade at this point in the war. *Oblt.* Ernst von Althaus and *Lt.* von Hartmann were brought in as replacements the next week.[48]

Boelcke left for an extended home leave on the evening of 21 May immediately after he had polished off his 18th victory. The next day, while in Kötthen awaiting his train for Dessau, few people recognized him at first because he had buttoned his overcoat all the way up to cover his *Pour le Mérite* (which according to its statutes was mandated to be worn "at all times"). The word soon got out, however, and the crowd that eventually gathered gave him a rousing send-off that, according to one witness, brought tears to everyone's eyes including Boelcke's.[49] Boelcke had another reason to feel uplifted that day. While walking through Kötthen, he had spotted a news summary posted in a shop window that announced that the Kaiser had promoted him to *Hauptmann* as a result of his 18th victory.

Boelcke's leave ended on 1 June and he returned to Sivry. On 18 June, English, American and French newspapers reported that he had been shot down three days earlier by French aviator Roger Ribiere.[50]

Above: Boelcke (third from right) marches in the procession that escorted *Oblt*. Max Immelmann's coffin to Douai rail station.

The story was retracted on 21 June, however, when American airman Lt. Victor Chapman testified that he had been shot up and given a glancing head wound while tangling with Boelcke on 17 June.[51] It is interesting to note that even though these reports appeared in foreign newspapers, Boelcke soon learned of his alleged demise at Ribiere's hands and mentioned the tale in a letter home dated 4 July 1916.

Ironically, on the very same day that the erroneous report of Boelcke's death was first published in Allied newspapers (18 June 1916), it was his former comrade, Max Immelmann, who was killed in combat. At the time, Boelcke was slotted to be placed in command of a *Staffel* of six Fokker fighters based at Sivry, a precursor to the *Jagdstaffeln* that would be formed in late 1916. Immelmann's demise, however, changed everything. After returning from Immelmann's memorial ceremonies, Boelcke was confronted with disquieting news: "I heard shortly afterwards that after Immelmann's death the Crown Prince said he would not let me fly again under any circumstances. The next day I reported to the chief [of Field Aviation] in Charleville and lo! my anticipations were exceeded in every respect. The chief made a long speech, the purport of which was that I was to sit in a glass case in Charleville; I was not to fly at all for the present, because my 'nerves' must be rested, but I could organize a Fokker *Staffel* in Charleville. Well, you can just imagine my rage! I was to sit in a cold water sanatorium in Charleville, stare up at the sky and take over the job of leading a crowd of weak-nerved pilots in need of rest!... I could only protest vigorously and then, knowing no better counsel, took my leave. When I got outside I cursed the adjutant and other pen-pushers in a most offensive fashion, which only, however, provoked mirth from all concerned. One of the fellows gave me a wise lecture to the effect that I was no longer a private individual who could play with his life at will but the property of the German nation, which still expected much from me. Finally, Captain Förster told me that for the present I was not to fly

Above: From left to right, Oswald Boelcke, *Lt.* Kurt Rackow, Crown Prince Wilhelm, *Oblt.* Cordt von Brandis – all holders of the *Orden Pour le Mérite*. The photo was taken at the Crown Prince's headquarters at Stenay around the time of Immelmann's death.

Above: Boelcke visited two German warships, SMS *Breslau* and SMS *Goeben*, on 17 July 1916 during his stay in Constantinople. "When I left, Captain Ackermann, the commanding officer of the *Goeben*, called for three cheers for me, and the sailors hoisted me up on their shoulders. What a lot of things they do for me!" (*Knight of Germany*, p.192; *Boelcke: der Mensch*, p.175)

any more – there was nothing doing there because it was a direct order from the Emperor, who had continually kept himself informed about me through the air chief. But if I had any other wish, I had only to express it; for example, I could go to Turkey and have a look at the other fronts."[52]

Boelcke indeed decided to tour the Balkans, Turkey and the Eastern Front. He managed to squeeze in his 19th victory on 27 June before being reminded in no uncertain terms that his flying ban was in full effect. Back in Berlin to prepare for his journey, he had lunch with the Kaiser: "...who greeted me with the words: 'You see, we have put you on the leash now!'...When I left, I met His Excellency von Falkenhayn in the courtyard; he also gloated over me – they are all pleased to have me sitting in a glass case."[53] After dining with Willy Aschenborn on 7 July, Boelcke left Berlin and then traveled through Vienna, Budapest, Belgrade and Sofia on his way to Istanbul, Turkey. From there he toured Smyrna and its surroundings before moving on to the Dardanelles, where he broke his flying ban and flew an *Eindecker* on several missions without encountering the enemy. He returned to Bulgaria on 2 August and then, after a brief stopover at Austrian General Headquarters at Teschen, went off to Kowel near the Eastern Front on 10 August. His purpose in going to Kowel was to visit with his brother Wilhelm, who was in command of *Kampfstaffel* 10 (part of *Kampfgeschwader* 2), located nearby. Once there, however, he learned that he was to report back to Germany to head up and organize *Jagdstaffel* 2, one of the first fighter units. Before departing, he famously invited two *KG* 2 pilots, *Lt.* Erwin Böhme and *Lt.* Manfred von Richthofen, to join his new unit. Brest Litovsk (where he visited with his old friend, Baltzer) and Warsaw were his next destinations before he went to Vilnius to meet up with brother Martin. Then came Berlin and finally Dessau on 20 August. Throughout his six week sojourn, Boelcke had been feted by generals and royalty as well as by members of local high society. He was also awarded at least three – and probably five – new decorations, which he characteristically never mentioned in his letters home. Those letters did reflect, however, that the times he enjoyed most were spent with his fellow servicemen in the army, navy and air services.

Left: This may be a photograph taken on 16 September 1916 when Boelcke and his men went to *Armee-Flug-Park* 1, commanded by *Hptm*. Alfred Keller, to collect their new Albatros fighters. Manfred von Richthofen smiles fourth from left, just behind Keller, as Boelcke peers at a leather document case.

The wealth of information that has been published regarding *Jagdstaffel* 2, Boelcke's first true fighter unit, will not be repeated here.[54] In brief, the unit was officially created as of 10 August (while Boelcke was away) and was first assembled at Vélu near Bertincourt (where *Jasta* 1 was based) on 27 August. Four permanent hangars had been left at Vélu airfield by its former occupant, *FFA* 32, but little else. Boelcke initially commanded only two officers other than himself (*Lt.* Hans-Joachim von Arnim and *Lt.* Wolfgang Gunther) and 64 service men, but no pilots or aircraft.[55] Eventually, both started trickling in. On 1 September, Anthony Fokker sent Boelcke two planes, D.III 352/16 and what appears to have been D.I 185/16 (see p.50 below), and *Fw.* Leopold Rudolf Reimann ferried an Abatros D.I over from *Jasta* 1. Boelcke used one or another from this small stable to shoot down an incredible total of seven enemy aircraft before a new batch of five Albatros D.Is and D.II 386/16 (which would serve as his personal aircraft from then on) arrived on 16 September. The next day, Boelcke flew with his men as a group for the first time and their success was immediate: first a victory for *Lt.* Erwin Böhme and then one each for Boelcke, *Lt.* Hans Reimann and *Lt.* Manfred von Richthofen. Boelcke had expressed his enjoyment in instructing men under his charge at *Telegraphen-Bataillon* Nr.3, and it was no different for *Jasta* 2: "My pilots are all passionately keen and very competent, but I must first train them to steady team-work – they are at present rather like young puppies in their zeal to achieve something." "I have to give my pilots some training. That is not so simple because they are all inspired with such fiery zeal that it is often difficult to put the brake on them. They have certainly learnt that the main thing is to get the enemy in your power and beat him down at once instead of arguing with him. But until I get it into their heads that everything depends on sticking together through thick and thin when the *Staffel* goes into battle and that it does not matter who actually scores the victory as long as the *Staffel* wins it – well, I can talk myself silly, and sometimes I have to turn my heavy batteries on to them. I always give them some instruction before every flight and especially after every flight. But they take it all very willingly." One can certainly sense his pride when he wrote on 17 September: "The *Staffel* is making itself! We have got five English machines since yesterday!"; and on 19 October: "We swept the board between Thiepval and Sars, i.e. we attacked and chased away every Englishman we found, no matter whether he was flying high or low... The total since September is thirty-seven victories, although we have had a lot of bad weather lately. They are really splendid, clever gentlemen – my *Staffel*!"[56]

Before this, however, while *Jasta* 2 was still being assembled, a somewhat rare occurrence took place at Vélu field. A well-known reporter from neutral America's "The New York World" newspaper, Herbert Bayard Swope, was permitted to interview Boelcke there sometime during 2–6 September.[57] Some excerpts: "His manner of thought is simple and direct, his conversation modest and responsive." "The English say the German fighters and observers

Above: American journalist Herbert Bayard Swope (far left) interviews Boelcke (center) at *Jasta* 2's Vélu airfield in early September 1916.

almost never cross their own lines, but fly over their own troops,' I said to Boelke [sic]. 'That isn't true as regards the observers,' he answered earnestly. 'They have done much good work over the enemy's forces, but it used to be true in part about the fighters. It was due at first to the fact that there were several parts of our new Fokkers we wanted to keep secret; second, because it was important that we remain on the ground in our own territory to prevent the enemy observers gaining information. Lastly, circumstances are changed, and we fly everywhere. Obviously it always is the best tactics to bring your man down behind your own lines so he can be made a prisoner if alive, and his machine kept from the enemy for repair. But each follows a fight through now, no matter where it takes us.'" The article also described Boelcke's encounter with his 20th victim, Capt. R.E. Wilson, and his invitation to have him dine at their mess. Curiously, Boelcke made a point of addressing another issue: "'Since you will write for America to read, you might straighten out one point. The London papers have credited me with saying I used to live in America, where I was a lift boy and got my flying experience in that way. I was never in America, and never happened to be a lift boy. I lived in Dessau, did some flying just a few months before the war began, liked the work, and when called out went into the flying branch. I hope to visit America for the first time after the war.'" Boelcke had first mentioned this false tale in a letter home dated 11 October 1915, so it had apparently continued to bother him for some time.

During Boelcke's tenure, *Jasta* 2 became the fighter training ground for such noted aces as Erwin Böhme, Hans Imelmann, Stefan Kirmaier, Erich König, Max Müller, Leopold Rudolf Reimann and, of course, Manfred von Richthofen. In September alone, *Jasta* 2 mounted 186 sorties that resulted in 69 combats and 25 victories. By the time of Boelcke's death on 28 October 1916, the unit had amassed 54 victories (21 of them his) with *Jasta* 1's 20 and *Jasta* 4's 19 as the closest competitors. The second highest scoring German ace with 19 total victories was Kurt Wintgens of *Jasta* 1, but he had been shot down and killed on 25 September. Then came Wilhelm Frankl from *Jasta* 4 with 15 – tied with Boelcke's former comrade-in-arms, the late Max Immelmann. But Boelcke stood apart from them all as the war's "Ace of Aces" with an incredible score of 40 victories.

The cumulative effect of two years of fighting and new command responsibilities eventually caught up with Boelcke. On 22 September 1916, when *Jasta* 2 moved to its new forward airfield at Lagnicourt, Boelcke was almost left behind because of a serious "asthmatic complaint" at least partially brought on by stress. He refused to go to the hospital, however, and doggedly returned to flying five days later. Boelcke's orderly, Ludwig Fischer (who remained on close personal terms with the Bölcke family after Oswald's death), related: "'My captain kept on growing thinner and more serious... The superhuman burden of seven take-offs a day for fights and the worries about his *Staffel* weighed him down. General von Below, the commander-in-chief of our army, wanted to send him on leave because he was overworked, but he would not go... He was always cheerful when he came back from a victory with the *Staffel*, but otherwise he was often in a very depressed mood in the last few days.'"[58] The evening before his death, he left the officer's mess and returned to his quarters complaining that there was too much noise for him. He asked Fischer to play a recording of "Father, Mother, Sisters, Brothers Have I in the World No More" and listened to it staring into the fire. *Lt.* Erwin Böhme, almost twelve years his senior and the man that Richthofen identified as "the one perhaps closest to Boelcke," later joined him in quiet conversation until Fischer suggested it was time to retire for the evening.[59]

On 28 October 1916, Boelcke took off on the first of the day's sorties around 7:00 a.m. in response to a report of enemy aircraft in the

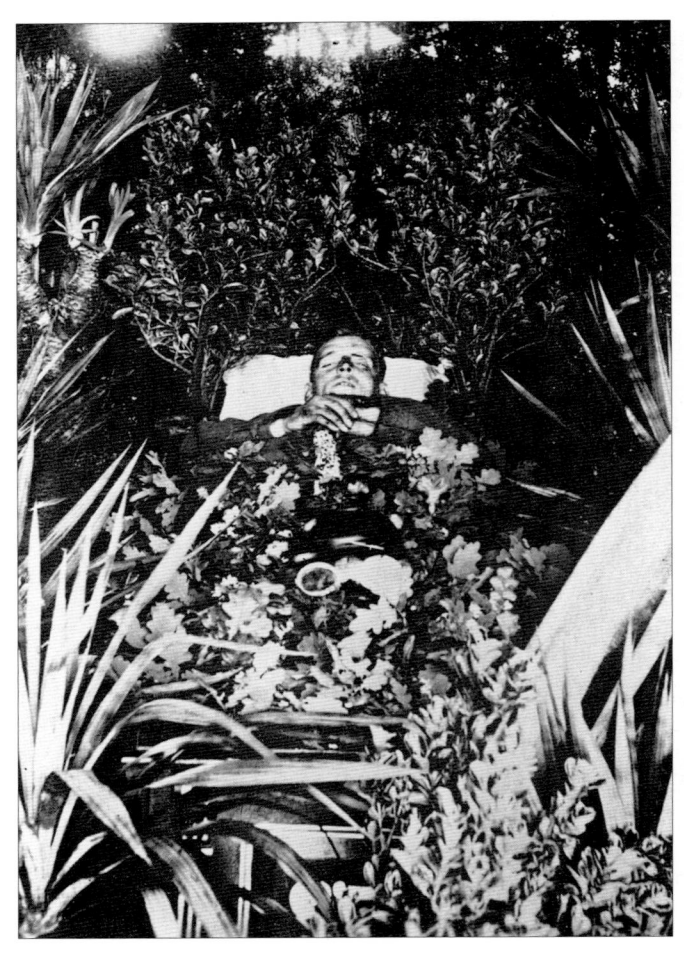

Above: Boelcke's remains lie in state at Lagnicourt airfield before being taken to Cambrai cathedral.

vicinity. At some point after his return, *Hptm.* von Gleichen-Russwurm brought *Hptm.* Walter Bloem to Lagnicourt field to meet Boelcke (Gleichen-Russwurm was from Dessau and had recently befriended Boelcke). What follows are excerpts from an article Bloem wrote that was published in the 11 November 1916 edition of *Die Woche* (46, pp.1605-07): "A harsh, blustery, overcast, late autumn morning. Rain squalls broke over Picardy's barren plateau in sudden outbursts from the southwest, and the four-month battle roiled and and thundered around us incessantly... we climbed up to the fighter unit's airfield through the awful autumn mud that rushed over the worn-out roadway like a broad stream of milk chocolate. A familiar sight: the roomy tents for the machines fluttered and rattled in the autumn windstorm; before them, the squadron's eight machines assembled in a long line with their noses to the wind, ready for flight; on the edge of the meadow a row of low wooden shacks made from rough pine planks. We knocked on the door of the shack that some industrious mechanics in field-gray had indicated was their leader's residence. A bright, steely voice invited us to enter. There stood the young warrior, the Ruler of the Skies, at his desk, telephone to his ear in an official discussion that gave us time to examine his features. A noticeably compact figure, a small but powerful body in a fur-lined, short flying coat, brown field boots and gray puttees. A stocky neck and distinguished-looking smallish head with a beardless, still quite youthful face; a strong, prominent nose underneath a slender forehead; a somewhat broad, imperious mouth. Then the long-distance call was over and a stocky, strong hand reached out to us for a powerful handshake. The mouth flashed a comradely smile and a pair of blue eyes, in which the true essence of this man are expressed, sparkled at us. It can't be helped – the old expression 'eagle eyes' must be used here. It is the only way to describe the strangely piercing, 'light beacon' as it were of their gaze... Boelcke said, 'We combat pilots have the job of looking for the enemy and attacking him whenever we find him. Others of our comrades have different duties, very difficult and important duties, that require the greatest devotion and self-sacrifice: the artillery spotting fliers, the infantry fliers, etc. It's a real shame that the public only knows something about us combat pilots. As a result, all young men want to be combat pilots, to earn the *Pour le Mérite* and make a name for themselves. Yet flying is done not only for fighting and shooting down enemy aircraft, but also for reconnaissance, observation and so forth. These tasks are the true purpose of flying. Combat pilots only have the job of protecting their comrades who are really working usefully and of destroying the enemy by effective flying work. It should be publicized that the really important types of fliers are only allowed to fight in self-defense and thus do not have the opportunity of being mentioned in the army reports as often as we are.'" Bloem's party wanted to continue talking with Boelcke for hours more, but realized he was a busy man with other duties. So they left and wished him luck. "That evening, in a high staff officer's office building, we were met with the crushing news: Boelcke is dead."

Boelcke had gone up on his sixth sortie of the day a little after 4:30 p.m., joined by Böhme and Richthofen. Both his companions' accounts of what ensued have often been reprinted elsewhere. To summarize, while chasing after the same plane, Böhme's undercarriage struck the upper left wing of Boelcke's D.II, causing a piece of it to break away. Boelcke struggled to bring the plane under control but was killed when the plane inevitably returned to earth. In a letter to his fiancée, Böhme concluded: "Boelcke never wore a crash helmet and

Above: Boelcke's coffin (center right) rests on a horse-drawn gun carriage in front of Cambrai Cathedral before the procession to the rail station. Prof. Max Bölcke and his wife (center) stand on the cathedral steps wearing black mourning clothes.

Right: Manfred von Richthofen (far right), carrying Boelcke's *Ordenskissen*, leads the procession into Cambrai rail station.

also did not buckle himself firmly into his Albatros. Otherwise, he might have survived the actually not powerful impact."[60] Richthofen, in a letter home to his mother, further elaborated that Boelcke's skull had been crushed upon impact.[61] Historians have been puzzled by these notations because they imply that Boelcke had hit the butt of one of his machine guns (which both protruded into the cockpit); yet there is no evidence of frontal lobe or facial damage in his open casket photo. A lesser-known

Above: Boelcke's coffin is placed on a catafalque at Cambrai rail station as his mourners gather for the farewell ceremony.

eyewitness account from a soldier on the ground clears the matter up: "Thus he lost lateral steering control, which was instantly noticeable because he immediately began to go into spiralling turns and with great skill came down to about 500 meters altitude. He wanted to land near Bapaume, but a side gust denied him the ability to select his own landing place because the damaged machine could barely obey its pilot. So he had to set down in soggy clay soil where he could not let his plane taxi and the machine turned vertically on its head, whereby Boelcke sustained a mortal injury to the back of his head. The resolute calm that was otherwise on his features was disturbed only a little…"[62] We now know then that the wheels of Boelcke's Albatros had dug into the muddy ground and flipped the plane over, fracturing the back of his skull.

Two services were held in Boelcke's honor and both were conducted on a massive scale. The first was held at Cambrai Cathedral (over the initial objections of local French authorities) where the plain wood coffin containing Boelcke's body was placed on a catafalque before the altar, flanked by tall candles and an honor guard. It soon became obscured, however, by the multitude of wreaths and flowers sent by his mourners. On the morning of 31 October 1916, Boelcke's parents and three of his brothers first visited with the men of *Jasta* 2 at Lagnicourt before moving on to Cambrai. There they encountered hundreds of military personnel lining the street and the main entrance of the cathedral. Inside, the coffin was now draped in Imperial Germany's colors with an aviator's crash helmet placed on top; and Boelcke's decorations were displayed before it on the black satin pillow called an *Ordenskissen*. The memorial ceremony began at 3 p.m. with Divisional Chaplain Selter presiding. The host of high-ranking dignitaries in attendance included Crown Prince Rupprecht of Bavaria, *Gen.* Fritz von Below (the Kaiser's representative), *Gen.* Sixt von Arnim and *Gen.* Wolf Marschall von Altengottern. Chaplain Selter led them all in prayer and song and delivered a eulogy. Then, headed by Manfred von Richthofen carrying Boelcke's *Ordenskissen*, the coffin was taken outside and borne down the cathedral steps. As it was loaded onto a black-draped gun carriage in front of the Bölcke family, several airplanes flew overhead in salute. The procession, assembled with Richthofen and Boelcke's *Ordenskissen* again in front, followed the horse-drawn gun carriage along Cambrai's streets to the rail station. Once there, the coffin was placed on another raised platform in front of four flaming, black obelisks and encircled by the mourners. After *Gen.* von Below and *Oblt.* Stefan Kirmaier, Boelcke's replacement as CO of *Jasta* 2, delivered lauditory addresses, Boelcke's coffin was loaded onto a train and three volleys were fired into the air in final tribute. When all was ready, the train pulled slowly out of the station with the strains of the military lament *"Ich hatt' ein Kameraden"* playing in the background. As Richthofen himself observed, the

Above: An aerial view, taken from one of the aircraft flying overhead in salute, of Boelcke's funeral procession as it wends it way through Dessau to the war dead cemetery.

Above: Boelcke's coffin, covered with wreaths and flowers, at his final resting place in Dessau's war dead cemetery.

memorial service had been "like that of a reigning prince."[63]

The train made its way back to Germany and stopped briefly in Magdeburg where solemn music and a flyover by pilots from the nearby Halberstadt flight school – where Boelcke had received his initial flight training – honored his memory. It reached Dessau station around 8 p.m. on 1 November where, despite the lateness of the hour, many of the city's officials and citizens greeted it. An honor guard consisting of men from the Air Service and the local garrison was formed and the coffin placed on a carriage. With Martin carrying his brother's *Ordenskissen* behind the carriage, and the remainder of the family riding in a car behind him, Boelcke's remains were borne throught the streets of Dessau accompanied by mourners carrying torches to light the way. When the coffin arrived at St. John's Church, it was placed before the altar while organ music quietly played in the background and remained there all night with an NCO pilot honor guard keeping watch. The next day, 2 November, the spot was again inundated with wreaths, flowers and other decorations from the Kaiser, the Duke and Duchess of Anhalt, military personnel and others wishing to pay tribute to the deceased airman. Then Boelcke's funeral service commenced at 3:45 p.m. led by Pastor Finger, who had given Boelcke his confirmation rites years earlier in the same church. *Gen.* Moritz von Lyncker, the Kaiser's representative, delivered the eulogy and Pastor Finger led the mourners in the closing prayer service. As the coffin was carried out of the church, it was met by what seemed to be the entire populace of Dessau, all dressed in mourning attire. They lined the way to the new war dead's Honor Cemetery and took part in delegation after delegation in the long procession that bore Oswald Boelcke to his final resting place. Once again, aircraft flew overhead, sometimes silencing their engines in salute to their fallen comrade. Friedrich II, Duke of Anhalt, awaited Boelcke's remains at the cemetery entrance and followed them in as they were carried to an isolated spot and placed on a dais there. Pastor Finger and Dessau's mayor, Dr. Eberling, gave their addresses before *Oberstleutnant* Hermann Thomsen, now Chief of Staff of the *Luftstreitkräfte* (Air Force), stepped before the crowd. He delivered a stirring speech, later published throughout Germany, that proclaimed that all German airmen must aspire to the solemn vow: "I will be a Boelcke!" Pastor Karl Boelcke (Oswald's uncle) spoke the final words of blessing for his nephew and the ceremony concluded with three volleys of gunfire.

It was subsequently decreed that fresh laurel wreaths from the Air Force would adorn Boelcke's grave at each anniversary of his death. This indeed took place the following year. *GenLt.* Ernst von Hoeppner, Commanding General of the Air Force, sent a delegation of 25 airmen to Dessau on 28 October 1917. Included among them was *Lt.* Erwin Böhme – the man who had played a tragic role in Boelcke's accident – who was now *Jasta* Boelcke's CO and placed that unit's tribute upon the grave. As we shall see later in this series, Böhme joined his friend in death a month and a day after this anniversary tribute.

Endnotes
[1] Though the rest of the family used the spelling, "Bölcke," Oswald preferred and adopted the latinized version, "Boelcke."
[2] Rolf Sommer, *Fliegerhauptmann Oswald Boelcke.* p.7.
[3] Werner, *Knight of Germany*, p.2; *Boelcke: der Mensch*, p.8.
[4] Luebke, *Hauptmann Boelcke†*, p.8.

[5] *Fliegerhauptmann Oswald Boelcke*, p.11.
[6] *Fliegerhauptmann Oswald Boelcke*, p.8.
[7] *Knight of Germany*, p.6; *Boelcke: der Mensch*, p.11.
[8] "*Als Beobachter Boelckes im Westen*" pp.216–17.
[9] *Knight of Germany*, pp.14–15; *Boelcke: der Mensch*, pp.18–19.
[10] *Knight of Germany*, p.20; *Boelcke: der Mensch*, p.24.
[11] *Knight of Germany*, pp.24, 32–34; *Boelcke: der Mensch*, pp.27–28, 34–35.
[12] *Knight of Germany*, p.45; *Boelcke: der Mensch*, p.46.
[13] *Knight of Germany*, p.52; *Boelcke: der Mensch*, p.52. *Fliegerbataillon* Nr.3 was based at Griesheim, adjacent to where Boelcke's telegraph unit was located.
[14] Boelcke suffered engine failure during his solo flight and was forced to land in a cornfield, where the plane ended up resting on its nose with a broken propeller.
[15] *Knight of Germany*, pp.60–61; *Boelcke: der Mensch*, pp.59–60.
[16] *Knight of Germany*, p.62; *Boelcke: der Mensch*, p.60.
[17] *Knight of Germany*, p.80; *Boelcke: der Mensch*, p.76.
[18] *Knight of Germany*, p.78; *Boelcke: der Mensch*, p.74.
[19] Wilhelm's awards fell on 9 September (2nd Class) and 23 October 1914 (1st Class).
[20] *Knight of Germany*, p.84; *Boelcke: der Mensch*, p.79.
[21] *Boelcke: der Mensch*, p.80. This writer's translation is somewhat different than that offered in *Knight of Germany*, p.84.
[22] *Knight of Germany*, p.84; *Boelcke: der Mensch*, p.80. Boelcke states that the only reason he went to the hospital in Château-Porcien was because he hoped to find it easier to transfer to another *Abteilung* from there. Indeed, while there he was permitted to ride nine miles to Rethel to post a letter home; so one must question how authentic his alleged condition was.
[23] "*Als Beobachter Boelckes im Westen*," p.215.
[24] Ibid.
[25] *Knight of Germany*, p.100; *Boelcke: der Mensch*, p.93.
[26] "*Als Beobachter Boelckes im Westen*," p.217.
[27] *Knight of Germany*, pp.109–12; *Boelcke: der Mensch*, pp.101–03. The victims were *Lts.* Maurice Têtu and Georges de la Rochefoucauld from *Escadrille* MS15.
[28] "*Als Beobachter Boelckes im Westen*," pp.217–18.
[29] *Knight of Germany*, p.115; *Boelcke: der Mensch*, pp.106–07.
[30] *Knight of Germany*, p.116; *Boelcke: der Mensch*, p.107.
[31] The "French monoplane" was probably a two-seat Morane-Saulnier flown by the English. For Immelmann's account of this engagement, see p.68 below.
[32] *Boelcke: der Mensch*, pp.109-10. Note: This writer's translation differs from the one offered by *Knight of Germany*, pp.118–19 where it is incorrectly stated that they went up in Immelmann's machine and that Immelmann had never fired the machine gun before his first victory.
[33] For example, see Norman Franks, Frank Bailey and Russell Guest, *Above the Lines* (Grub Street, 1993); Trevor Henshaw, *The Sky Their Battlefield* (Grub Street, 1995); Norman Franks and Hal Giblin, *Under the Guns of the German Aces* (Grub Street, 1997); Norman Franks, *Sharks Among Minnows* (Grub Street, 2001); Greg VanWyngarden, *Early German Aces of World War I* (Osprey, 2006).
[34] This writer has seen several unpublished private communications from both Boelcke and Immelmann. Judging from them and those already available, it seems that Boelcke sometimes was annoyed by Immelmann's willingness to promote his fame (by encouraging various postcard publications and their sale). For example, Boelcke wrote on the back of one Immelmann postcard: "*Findet Ihr das schön? Ich nicht!*" ("Do you find this nice? I don't!"); yet he wrote something similar on the back of one of his own (see p.19.) Overall, they seemed to respect one another – though perhaps Immelmann moreso regarding Boelcke than vice versa. In fact, Immelmann wrote very pleasant, complimentary letters to Boelcke's father.
[35] This was the covert name of a newly-formed bombing squadron that later became designated as *Kampfgeschwader* 2.
[36] *Knight of Germany*, pp.121–22; *Boelcke: der Mensch*, pp.111–12.
[37] Thies, *Auktion Nachlass Oswald Boelcke*, p.172. Curiously, *Boelcke: der Mensch* (pp.112–13) paraphrased this passage in Boelcke's prior letter dated 9 September 1915. To add to the confusion, *Knight of Germany* (p.122) then misdated the letter as 9 August 1915.
[38] Thies, *Auktion Nachlass Oswald Boelcke*, pp.240–41.
[39] There were also 22 bestowals of the *Pour le Mérite* with Oakleaves, a higher level of the award for men already holding its regular version. and were among the 70 cited above. Of these, 19 were to generals, two to royalty and one to an admiral.
[40] *Knight of Germany*, pp.114–15; *Boelcke: der Mensch*, p.106.
[41] *Knight of Germany*, p.131; *Boelcke: der Mensch*, p.121.
[42] *Boelcke: der Mensch*, p.134. This writer's translation is slightly different than that found in *Knight of Germany*, p.145. Boelcke's allusion to a "sheet of questions and answers" referred to a humorous leaflet he jokingly distributed in early 1915 to "troublesome questioners" in anticipation of their oft-repeated inquiries (see *Knight of Germany*, p.87; *Boelcke: der Mensch*, p.82).
[43] *Knight of Germany*, p.148; *Boelcke: der Mensch*, p.136.
[44] *Knight of Germany*, pp.164–65; *Boelcke: der Mensch*, p.151.

[45] We know that Boelcke owned a *Grossordenschnalle* (full dress medals bar) because it was displayed at his funeral. He may have been required to wear it at certain military ceremonies, but it is clear he rarely, if ever, did in public.
[46] *Knight of Germany*, p.151; *Boelcke: der Mensch*, p.139. The other small fighter contingent was established at Avillers.
[47] *Knight of Germany*, pp.157-58; *Boelcke: der Mensch*, pp.144–45. The first machine with a cannon had been brought down intact by Wilhelm Frankl on 10 January 1916 as his second victory.
[48] This was the same *Lt.* von Hartmann who later served in *Jasta* 11 and appeared in several famous April/May 1917 photos of the unit.
[49] Gottschalk, *Boelcke† Deutschlands Fliegerheld* pp.76–80.
[50] E.g., see *The New York Times*, June 18 1916.
[51] *The New York Times*, June 21 1916.
[52] *Knight of Germany*, pp.180–81; *Boelcke: der Mensch*, pp.165–66.
[53] *Knight of Germany*, p.182; *Boelcke: der Mensch*, p.167.
[54] For example, see Norman Franks, *Jasta Boelcke* (Grub Street, 2004) or Greg VanWyngarden, *Jagdstaffel 2 'Boelcke'* (Osprey, 2007).

[55] While awaiting the delivery of *Jasta* 2 aircraft, Arnim returned to his former unit, *AFA* 207, for one last mission in which he was killed by Lt. Albert Ball on 28 August.
[56] *Knight of Germany*, pp.209, 212, 213, 223; *Boelcke: der Mensch*, pp.190, 192, 193, 202.
[57] For a complete transcript of the Swope article and its later appearance as a chapter in one of his books, see *Over The Front* 17:3, pp.261–73.
[58] *Knight of Germany*, p.227; *Boelcke: der Mensch*, p.205.
[59] Richthofen, *The Red Baron*, p.58; *Der Rote Kampfflieger*, p.111.
[60] *Over The Front* 5:1, pp.48–49. Werner, *Briefe eines deutschen Kampffliegers*, p.71.
[61] Fischer, *Mother of Eagles*, p.105; Richthofen, *Mein Kriegstagebuch*, p.86.
[62] *Die Luftflotte* 12, p.172.
[63] Fischer, *Mother of Eagles*, p.105; Richthofen, *Mein Kriegstagebuch*, p.86.

Right: Here we see Boelcke climbing out of the pilot's cockpit of a Roland C.II. It is assumed he had just flown this aircraft, perhaps to assess its characteristics. The time and place of the photo are unknown, but we know the C.II began making it to the Front in early 1916.

Boelcke – The Aircraft

Bristol-*Taube*
(June – early August 1914)

By his own account, Oswald Boelcke's pilot training occurred in early June 1914 in "70 PS-Bristol-*Tauben*" ("70 hp Bristol-*Taubes*") at an airfield outside Halberstadt.[1] A company initially named "Deutsche Bristol-Werke Flugzeug GmbH" had been formed there on 9 April 1912 to produce aircraft conforming to the British and Colonial Aeroplane Company, Ltd.'s Bristol Boxkite and Coanda designs. Bristol-Werke, later called "Halberstädter Flugzeugwerke Gmbh," branched out into producing a series of "*Taube*" monoplanes powered by 70, 75 and 100 hp engines.[2] Little is known about the precise nature of these aircraft, but it is speculated that they were probably similar to Bristol's Coanda design that served as a stable two-seat trainer and sported a four-wheeled undercarriage. Boelcke arrived at Halberstadt on 2 June and reported flights in 70 and 100 hp *Taubes* (including his first solo in a 70 hp model on 3 July) up through early August.

Aviatik Biplane (B.I?)
(August 1914)

After the war broke out, Boelcke was sent to Darmstadt to serve in a *Flieger-Ersatz-Abteilung* where he not only earned his pilot's license on 15 August but also helped train new pilots in what he called an "Aviatik-*Doppeldecker*" ("Aviatik biplane").[3] In all likelihood he was referring to the Aviatik B.I that appeared in 1914 (the B.II was not introduced until 1915) and was powered by a 100 hp Mercedes D I engine.

Albatros Biplane B.I 176
(30 August 1914 – April 1915)

On 30 August Boelcke reported to *Etappen-Flugzeugpark* 4 near Trier to await orders for further disposition to the Front. He was hoping to go to his older brother Wilhelm's unit, *Feldflieger-Abteilung* 13, and therefore practiced flying an "Albatros-*Doppeldecker*" ("Albatros biplane") – the only type flown by *FFA* 13 at the time.[4] This most likely was the Albatros B.I, initially developed before the war and then adapted for reconnaissance and flight

B1: Oswald Boelcke poses in the aft cockpit of an Albatros B.I while his brother stands alongside. The tail's vertical stabilizer carries the serial number "176" (which appears to have been applied in the field) while the rudder bears a somewhat crudely-painted cross pattée against a white square. Large cross pattées against white squares were painted on both wings' upper surfaces, and it is assumed that this was repeated on their lower surfaces as well. Note that they are positioned considerably more inboard than seen later on in the war. The vertical stabilizer and rudder are not of the typical design seen on many Albatros B.Is and are more reminiscent of the style used later on the B.III. B-model aircraft usually situated the pilot in the rear cockpit and the observer in the forward one. Their positions were reversed, however, when the C-models armed with machine guns were created and the aft cockpit provided the observer with a better field of fire.

B2: Boelcke stands on a crate in front of what is probably the same plane seen in B1. Presumably, the men with him were his mechanics.

training duties when the war began. After a bit of finagling (see p.10 above), Boelcke indeed joined his brother at *FFA* 13's base at La Ferté-sur-Chiers on 31 August; and the next day, he and Wilhelm took off on their first wartime reconnaissance flight together. As the front lines surged back and forth, *FFA* 13 changed air bases from La Ferté to Buzancy, Chatel-Chéhéry, Sainte-Menehould, back to Buzancy, and finally Pontfaverger-Moronvilliers on 20 September 1914. The brothers remained together at Pontfaverger until Wilhelm's transfer to another unit on 4 April 1915. Boelcke's biography gives no indication that they flew together in any other biplane than "his" (i.e., Oswald's) throughout this period.[5] Though it nevertheless remains possible that they may have occasionally flown in different *FFA* 13 Albatros B.Is, Oswald's is probably the one included in his biography and labeled: "With his brother Wilhelm at Pontfaverger" (B1). Oswald is standing in the pilot's aft cockpit while Wilhelm leans against the plane next to him, wearing the Iron Cross 1st class that he received on the evening of 23 October 1914.[6] The horizontal stabilizer bears the number "176." This appears to be the same plane captured in another photo (B2) with Boelcke posing alongside it.

Fokker A.I/M.8
(8 December 1914 – April 1915)
While the Boelcke brothers were carrying out their reconnaissance duties in Oswald's Albatros biplane, Oswald began displaying overt signs of the fighter pilot he would eventually become. His biographer, Prof. Johannes Werner, reported: "... Lieut. Parschau, a Darmstadt acquaintance, paid a visit to Pontfaverger on Nov. 11th, 1914, with his small Fokker *Eindecker*.[7] Boelcke decided that he must have such a machine, and he went to Rethel on November 26th to obtain one. "I am sorry to say that I did not get my Fokker, because the only one there was reserved for another officer. But they have ordered me a new machine from the factory. I am delighted, as the Fokker's speed, climbing capacity and manageability make it very suitable for artillery spotting and short flights. When a favorable hour comes, we can use it, whereas we have to have at least two hours good weather with our old machine, because it climbs so slowly." – And in his entry of Dec. 9th: "I got my Fokker from Rethel yesterday. It is a monoplane, with a French rotary engine located forward; it is about half the size of a *Taube*... I got into it straight away in Rethel and flew here – it goes wonderfully in the air and is very easy to fly. So now I have two machines – the big biplane for longer flights and the little Fokker for artillery flights, etc. Both my children are now resting peacefully together in one tent – as it was difficult to make room for them both, the small one is dug in a bit, with his tail under the big fellow's wing. The Fokker is my big Christmas present, about which I am as delighted as a child."[8]

Boelcke's 10 December entry related that he flew Wilhelm to Rethel in the new Fokker and also gave several other men, including his orderly, rides

B3: This photo appeared in a 1916 publication entitled *Hauptmann Bölckes Feldberichte*. It has Wilhelm (left) and Oswald Boelcke (right) in front of a Fokker A.I/M.8 *Eindecker*. Though the book's caption states it was taken in September 1914, Boelcke's own correspondence coupled with the fact that the first A.I/M.8s were not delivered until October 1914 confirm that this was not the case. The Fokker A.I/M.8 was an improved version of the M.5 artillery spotter. Its wings were mounted high on the "shoulder" of the plane with large apertures covered by clear windscreens beneath them on both sides of the fuselage to enhance downward viewing. It carried two crewman who usually sat in tandem, or occasionally side-by-side in the cockpit.

in it. A photo (B3) originally published in 1916's *Hauptmann Bölcke's Feldberichte* (opp. p.32) shows Oswald (carrying his flight gear) and Wilhelm standing in front of what looks like a Fokker A.I/M.8 model *Eindecker*.[9] There is little doubt then that this was his "new Fokker."

LVG B.I 308
(Early May 1915)

On 4 April, the same day that brother Wilhelm had been transferred to a *Flieger-Ersatz-Abteilung* in Posen, Oswald came down with a bronchial condition (real or feigned, see p.11 above) and was sent to a hospital in Château-Porcien to recover. He remained there until the 18th and then rejoined *FFA* 13 at its new base at Warmeriville – but only for one week, because on 25 April he learned that he was to go to *FFA* 62 at Döberitz. After his arrival, he was assigned LVG B.I 308 which he took on a test run over his hometown of Dessau. The LVG B.I, originally developed in 1913, was quickly pressed into service at the outbreak of the war. Though generally powered by a 100 hp Mercedes D-I engine, a 110 hp Benz engine was sometimes substituted instead. Boelcke and his observer, *Lt.* Willy Aschenborn, were unimpressed with the pre-war model and quickly sought a replacement, which they found on 12 May (see p.13 above).

LVG B.II 712/15
(12 May – 12 June 1915)

Prof. Werner briefly notes that Boelcke obtained "a newer type of machine (B.712) from Johannisthal." [10] B.712 was an LVG B.II, which had first been introduced in the spring of 1915. Similar in appearance to the B.I, it had a reduced wingspan and a more powerful 120 hp Mercedes D.II engine. Like its predecessor, the pilot rode in the aft cockpit behind the observer.

FFA 62 left Döberitz on 13 May and arrived at Pontfaverger two days later. After a brief stop, it moved on to Douai and began operations there, together with *FFA* 20, on 20 May 1915. On 25 May, an LVG C.I borrowed by *FFA* 20 reportedly forced an armed French machine to land behind German lines. Prof. Johannes Werner (Boelcke's postwar biographer) knew that Boelcke had a captured French machine gun mounted on his B.II 712/15 around this time and assumed it came from this captured plane.[11] In his letter dated 25 June, Immelmann confirms how Boelcke had converted his defenseless B.II into a fighting machine: "As you will have read in the paper, an enemy machine was forced to land near Douai. Our captain went off there and saw it carried a machine gun. He asked the authorities who are in charge of the spoils if he might have it, and he got it. Then the French machine gun was mounted in our speediest and best climbing machine, a small so-called L.V.G., under our captain's directions. Lieutenant Boelcke flew this little L.V.G..."[12]

Immelmann inherited this machine after the new LVG C.Is arrived at Douai, and the only photos we have of it were taken after that point (see p.88).

LVG C.I 162/15
(13 June – 6 July 1915)

The LVG C.I was the first operational German two-seater specifically designed to carry a machine gun into battle. As a result, the more powerful 150 hp Benz Bz.III engine was used to accomodate the added weight. Another change was that the observer was now situated in the aft cockpit behind the pilot so that he could have a wider field of fire. Five of the new C.I fighting machines were delivered to Douai in mid-June 1915. Boelcke was assigned 162/15 and practiced flying it on 13–14 June before taking it into combat for the first time on the 15th. Boelcke was so intent on the fighting capability of the machine that he immediately replaced his former observer, Aschenborn, with *Lt.* Heinz Hellmut von Wühlisch, who had been through a machine gun course. Together, they coerced several French machines into diving escapes but were frustrated in their attempts to actually shoot one down. Then something occurred on 23 June that sealed Boelcke's fate in becoming a fighter pilot. Anthony Fokker, accompanied by *Lt.* Otto Parschau, demonstrated two of Fokker's E.I monoplanes at Douai airfield in front of not only the men of *FFA* 62 and 20, but also no less a personage than Crown Prince Rupprecht of Bavaria. *Lt.* Max Immelmann, then a *Fähnrich* (officer candidate) with *FFA* 62, wrote: "We have just got two small one-seater fighters from the Fokker factory. The Crown Prince of Bavaria visited our aerodrome to see these new fighting machines and inspected us and Section 20. Director Fokker, the constructor of this fighter, was presented to him.

Fokker and a Lieutenant Parschau gave exhibition flights for him and fired at ground targets from the air. Fokker amazed us with his ability."[13]

Boelcke himself was much more reticent when he wrote his parents on 24 June: "Yesterday afternoon our commanding general, the Crown Prince of Bavaria, inspected our aerodrome. We now have a collection there of practically every type of machine that our aviation technique has evolved – two sections (20 and 62) and a squadron of fighting machines. The two sections fly the ordinary biplanes... the squadron of fighters has come along because there is more going on here than anywhere else on the western front. They have the most cunning sorts of buses, e.g. a huge fighter with two engines that carries three men and a special bombdropping device – a most colossal ship. Then there are five other fighters armed with machine guns; they are much bigger than the ordinary machine. Besides those there are some little Fokker monoplanes, also with machine guns – every sort of machine that you want, in fact."[15] Only his log book entry for 24 June betrayed the fact: "Trial flight in Fokker E."[16] Still, it was while flying in C.I 162/15 with *Lt.* von Wühlisch that Boelcke achieved his first victory a short time later on 4 July.

Fokker E.I 3/15
(24 June – August 1915)

As we saw above, Boelcke took his first flight in a Fokker E.I on 24 June 1915 – the day after the type had been demonstrated at Douai airfield by Fokker and Parschau. According to Parschau, who remained at Douai to help familiarize pilots with the new type, a total of five E.Is were delivered there during his stay. It is clear, however, that three of them eventually went elsewhere (Lille was one location).[17] Though Immelmann at first states on 17 July that "Fokker went away several days ago, but left a one-seat fighter behind" for Boelcke, his later letters clarify that the unit actually possessed two such fighters.[18] Boelcke also confirms that their group had two *Eindeckers* when he said that *FFA* 62 and 20 now had "some little Fokker monoplanes, also with machine guns" on 24 June and referred to Immelmann taking up "our other monoplane" on 1 August.[19] Prof. Werner, who had access to Boelcke's personal records, identified the one assigned to Boelcke as E.I 3/15. Shortly after Boelcke and Wühlisch's victory in LVG C.I 162/15, Boelcke switched over to his *Eindecker* almost exclusively.[20] The other E.I, by virtue of Immelmann's statement – "My old 80 h.p. Fokker (the machine with factory number E 13), in which I finished off my first five Englishmen..." – must have been E.13/15.[21] Though

B4 – 8: On 11 August 1915, Boelcke informed his parents: "*Lt.* von John, who is in hospital here with an injured knee, came along to visit me with two nursing sisters. As they were both so longing for a flight, I took them one after another for a jaunt above the aerodrome in my little monoplane, to the great joy of all the beholders." (*Knight of Germany*, p.119; *Boelcke: der Mensch*, p.110) B4–6 show Boelcke and Nurse Blanka sitting in an E.I. B7 has, from left to right: *Lt.* von John (note bandaged knee under trousers), Nurse Blanka, Boelcke, unidentified nurse, unidentified soldier. B8 shows Boelcke dressed identically with helmet and goggles but no flight coat in the cockpit of the same plane. The serial number just visible under the wing informs us that it was not E.3/15 but E.13/15 – the other of the two *FFA* 62 E.Is that was primarily used by Immelmann.

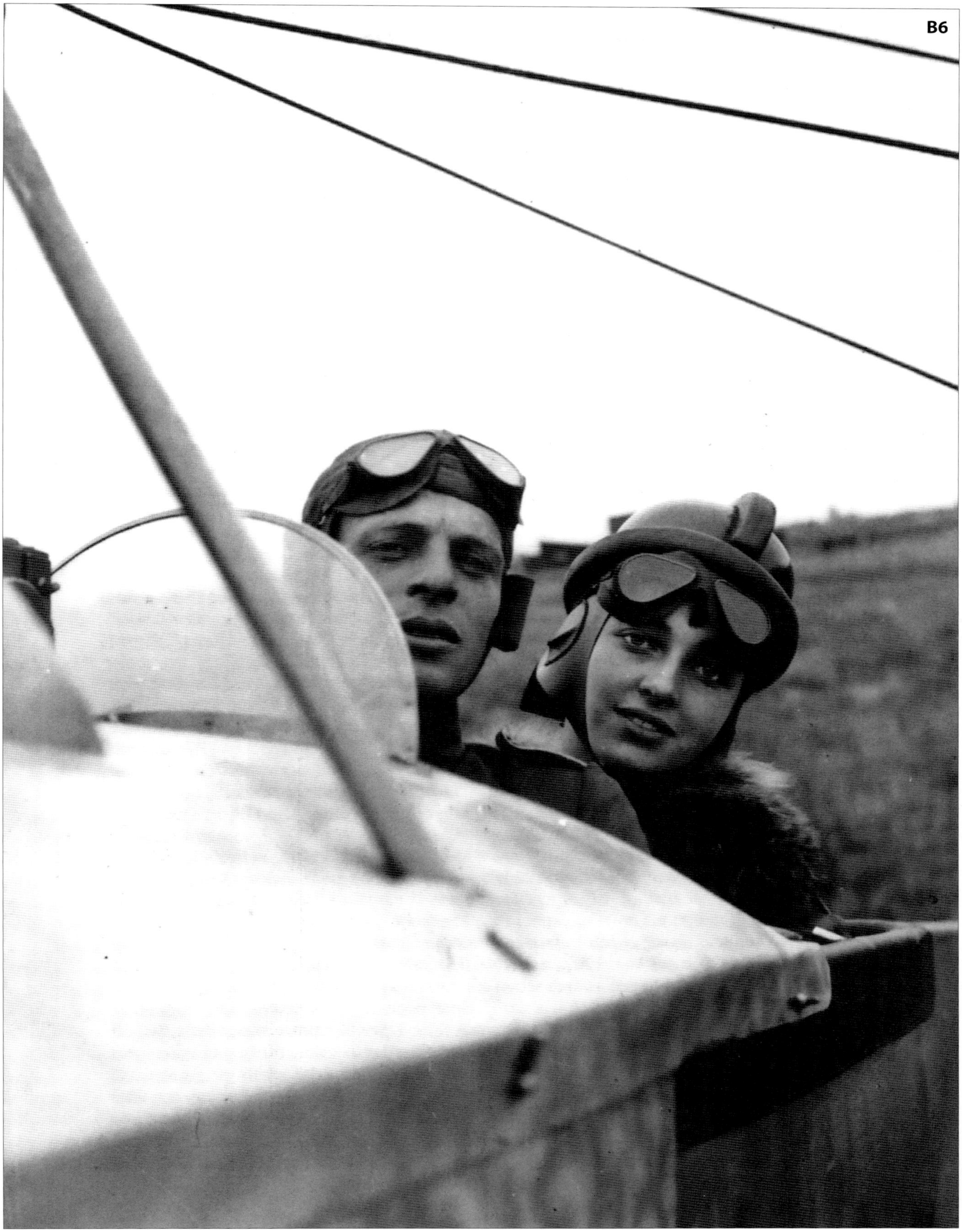
B6

B9: Judging by the snow on the ground and the heavy overcoat Boelcke is wearing, this photograph occurred in wintertime. He is posing in front of a Fokker fighter with a nine-cylinder engine that makes it either an E.II or E.III. We know that he flew a "fast, nimble Fokker" (probably an E.II or E.III) while serving with *B.A.M.* at Rethel (mid-October to early December 1915). After that, when he was transferred back to *FFA* 62, he had a 160 hp E.IV. Therefore, this may be a snapshot of Boelcke and the E.II/E.III he flew at Rethel before his return to Douai in December.

3/15 seems to have been Boelcke's primary mount, we have photographic evidence that he flew 13/15 on occasion as well (B4–B8). Unfortunately, this writer knows of no pictures of Fokker E.I 3/15.[22] While flying one of these E.Is, Boelcke achieved his second victory on 19 August.

Fokker *Übungsmaschine* (practice machine)
(30 July – 1915)
Max Immelmann was intrigued by the Fokker E.I and mentioned in his letter of 3 August 1915 that when Fokker left *FFA* 62 in July, he *"eine Übungsmaschine, d.h. eine ohne Maschinengewehr, hier gelassen"* ("had left a practice machine, i.e., one without a machine gun, here"). He went on to relate that on 30 July he asked Boelcke to take him up in it so that he could get a feel for its controls.[23] The exact model of this training machine is unknown, but we do know that the A.I/M.8 type was often used for this purpose at the time. Boelcke, already quite familiar with Fokker's rotary engine-powered monoplanes, probably rarely flew the practice machine, however.

Fokker E.II 37/15
(early – mid-September 1915)
Boelcke corresponded on 9 September 1915 that *"In der vorigen Woche habe ich eine interessante Reise machen können, da ich einen neuen Fokker bekommen sollte und mein alter schon fortgegeben war...Nun habe ich meinen neuen schönen Fokker E37 mit 100 PS, während mein früherer nur 80 hatte."* ("Last week I was able to make an interesting trip, since I needed to get a new Fokker and my older one had already been sent away... Now I have my new, beautiful Fokker E.37 with 100 h.p., whereas my earlier one only had 80.")[24] He wrote this the same day he bagged his third victim. Boelcke was not destined to enjoy 37/15 for very long though because Immelmann disclosed that shortly before Boelcke was informed of his transfer to *Brieftauben-Abteilung Metz* (*B.A.M.*) on 19 September, "Boelcke had bad luck with his 100 h.p. Fokker. Part of his engine broke away in the air, with the result that the cowling, the engine and the propeller went to pieces and he had to land. The machine was not serviceable again till three days ago."[25] After its repair, Immelmann took over E.II 37/15 (see p.90).

Unknown Fokker E.I, E.II or E.III
(late September – mid-October 1915)

Unknown Biplane
(perhaps late September – mid-October 1915)

Unnown Fokker E.II or E.III
(mid-October – early December 1915)
After Boelcke's arrival at *B.A.M.* on 21 September, he was slated to have "a biplane and a Fokker as well," but neither had arrived by the time the unit had relocated to Rethel in early October.[26] In the meantime, Boelcke used a borrowed "Fokker" to down his fourth official victory on 25 September. The precise model is unknown and could have been either an E.II, E.III or even an E.I. Writing from Rethel on 17 October, Boelcke mentions "I got my Fokker from Metz several days ago and flew it daily – to the great sorrow of Teubern, who consequently has nothing to do."[27] This statement implies that Boelcke and Teubern had flown together in a *B.A.M.* two-seater prior to this; but again, nothing is known about the type of plane. Boelcke used his recently-arrived Fokker (probably an E.II or E.III since it appears to have been a new machine and he referred to it as his "fast, nimble Fokker") to down

his fifth victim on 16 October as well as his sixth on 30 October. On 2 November, Boelcke stated: "By the way, in two or three weeks I am going to have a brand new Fokker again, with a more powerful engine (160 hp) and two machine guns."[28] Boelcke traveled to Schwerin to confer with Anthony Fokker on 11 November and perhaps to familiarize himself with the new 160 hp E.IV model that was coming his way. On 12 December, he was back writing letters from *FFA* 62 at Douai. Immelmann's 20 December correspondence reported: "...*seit etwa acht Tagen ist auch Boelcke wieder bei unserer Abteilung... Boelcke hat schon den 160 PS-Fokker, den ich mir in den nächsten Tagen holen soll.*" ("...Boelcke has been back at our *Abteilung* too for about eight days... Boelcke already has a 160 h.p. Fokker, which I am to get myself in the next few days.")[29]

Fokker E.IV 123/15
(mid-December 1915 – June 1916)

Aero historians have long sought to identify the precise serial number of Boelcke's first Fokker E.IV. We know that it came from the initial run of E.IVs designated 122–127/15, and many have favored either 122/15 or 123/15. Thanks to a previously unpublished photograph, the guesswork can now end (see B10 below). Under magnification, the serial number on the E.IV in the foreground – though partially obscured by a man's head – is "Fok...23..." Of all the serial numbers assigned to this model, "Fok.E IV 123/15" is the only possibility.[30] Three other things visible in the photograph confirm this identity as well. The cowling presents a fuller, pug-nose appearance than normally seen, the machine guns are offset to the starboard side of the nose as opposed to being centered on it, and the plane carries several large identification plates on and adjacent to the cowling. These are all distinct characteristics of the first two or three E.IVs to come off the production line (i.e., 122–124/15) that are not found on their successors.[31] But what then is the connection to Boelcke? The E.IV in the background sports a six-pointed star symbol on its wheel and is the same plane seen in another photo that displays the initials "OB" on its cowling (see B11 below). "OB" stood for "Oswald Boelcke" as attested to by other photos of his

B10 (top) & B10 Blowup (Above): This recent discovery is the key to confirming Boelcke's first E.IV as 123/15. The plane in the foreground displays all the unique characteristics of the first few E.IVs off the production line, and its partially-obscured serial number (see blowup) can only be matched to 123/15. The E.IV next to it is another of Boelcke's mounts seen in B11 and B26 as well. It bore his initials on its cowling (as did 123/15) and later had a six-pointed star applied to its wheels. This photo was taken at *Fokkerstaffel* Sivry in July or August 1916 after Boelcke had gone on a tour of the Eastern Front and left the planes behind.

B11 (B11 Blowup in inset): This is the same plane seen in the background of B10 (note the six-pointed star symbol on its wheel). Oswald Boelcke's stylized "OB" initials are clearly visible and match the design evident in B26. The man at left has alternately been identified as either *Hptm.* or *Maj.* von Essen. It is unknown at this time if he was a member of *Fokkerstaffel* Sivry.

B12: *FFA* 62 entertains a high-ranking visitor in late December 1915/early January 1916, showing him Oswald Boelcke's new Fokker E.IV 123/15. From left to right: *Lt.* von Seckendorf, *Hptm.* Hermann Kastner, Boelcke, *Gen.* Arnim von Holstein, *Lt.* Max Immelmann, *Lt.* Albert Oesterreicher and *Lt.* Ernst Hess.

B13: Boelcke sits in the cockpit of E.IV 123/15. The turtle deck forward of the cockpit has been removed to allow access to the guns which are clearly seen here as offset to starboard. The serial number's "E" is visible between the stepladder's legs.

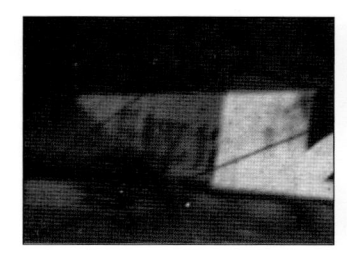

B14 Blowup (above)

aircraft. One of them (B26) shows Boelcke standing in the same E.IV's cockpit before the six-pointed star symbol was applied to its wheels and two others (B20, B25) demonstrate that a different-styled "OB" was once attached to 123/15's cowling.[32] So what this recent discovery displays are two of Boelcke's E.IV mounts together on one field – but as we shall soon see, they went through several transformations before getting there.

As we saw above, Oswald Boelcke expected his Fokker E.IV to arrive "two to three weeks" after 2 November. Fokker's records show that E.IV 123/15 left the factory in Schwerin on 26 November – a little later than Boelcke had thought.[33] After his return to *FFA* 62 at Douai on or around 12 December, Immelmann noted that Boelcke had his new Fokker on 20 December, and the next day Boelcke complained of "troubles with the new Fokker, occasioned by the fact that his mechanics were not yet familiar with the latest type."[34] B12 and B13 were taken at Douai around this time. Both show E.IV 123/15 in almost pristine condition. Boelcke's personal paint scheme – a broad white band around the fuselage centered on the national

B14: Boelcke takes off from Douai field in 123/15. The serial number was overpainted with Boelcke's white band marking and remained only partly visible (see blowup above). The plane has begun to show more signs of staining along the bottom of the fuselage and on the white band.

B16: E.IV 123/15 with a new paint job. Though the stained fuselage remained untouched, its white band has been repainted. The tri-color design on its wheels (believed to have been the German national colors of white, black and red) has also been added. Note the small clump of trees visible on the horizon. The same grouping can be seen in other photos taken at Sivry field (B18, B22).

B17–19: Three more shots (with a blowup of the last) of E.IV 123/15 with stained fuselage and comparatively clean white band. In B18, a Fokker E.II or E.III with distinctly styled crosses on its rudder and fuselage rests in the background. We have another picture of *Lt.* Werner Notzke and his mechanics posing in front of the same aircraft, so it presumably belonged to him (though it is not E.III 211/16 in which he died). Note too the clump of trees on the horizon to the left in B18. It is the same cluster visible in B16 and B22.

B15: Boelcke in front of 123/15. The fuselage displays even greater signs of staining, as does the wheel cover.

B20: Oswald Boelcke and his mechanics in front of 123/15. Compare the stylized initials on the cowling to those appearing on his later E.IV in B11. Note too another subtle difference between the first two E.IVs and subsequent ones: the cowling protrusions (at 0, 90 and 270 degrees) that covered three large engine mount bolts were pyramidal in shape on the prototypes whereas those on subsequent E.IVs were rectangular. For another picture of Boelcke's mechanics with this airplane, see p.59.

insignia – is evident. B14 captures Boelcke taking off in 123/15 at a later date, judging from the staining evident on the bottom of the fuselage and on the white band near the cross pattée. We can also see that the white band partially overpainted the plane's serial number, leaving "Fok EIV. 12..." with only half the '2' visible. The backs of at least two copies of this image identify it as Boelcke taking off from Douai airfield, which means that it probably occurred in January 1916 before his departure from *FFA* 62 on the 21st. From there, he went to Jametz to help escort *AFA* 203 aircraft conducting artillery spotting missions. While with *FFA* 62, Boelcke brought down his 7th–9th victims on 5, 12 and 14 January.

On 12 February 1916, Boelcke wrote from Jametz: "I have only flown four or five times since I have been here. It is not worth while to take off, as the French do not come across any more."[35] Later that month, Boelcke contracted "some stupid intestinal trouble" and was sent to a hospital in Montmédy.[36] B15 has Boelcke posing in front of 123/15 and seems to show even more staining on the white band near the national insignia. Boelcke is wearing a heavy overcoat (though not as heavy as the one seen in B9, B12–13), so we can conclude that it was probaby taken in late winter/early spring – perhaps at Jametz.

Frustrated with all the inactivity, Boelcke pressed his superiors to allow him to establish an airfield closer to the front lines. Permission was granted and he personally scouted out and chose a flat meadow near Sivry-sur-Meuse as his new base. He moved there on 11 March and brought along one other Fokker pilot: *Lt.* Werner Notzke. B16 has Boelcke sitting in the cockpit of 123/15, and several copies state the location was Sivry. Though the fuselage displays considerable staining, the white band seems freshly painted; so too the new tri-color design that now appears on the plane's wheel(s). The implication is that 123/15 received a new, partial paint job around the time of Boelcke's relocation to Sivry. The plane has a similar appearance in B17–20.

On 16 March, Boelcke wrote: "So I have had a lot of success with my 160 h.p. machine in the last few days, but a lot of trouble too. I got quite close to French machines behind our own lines on several occasions, but they escaped me because my engine was not in order. I am to have a new machine within the next few days – I hope business will be better then."[37] A little over one week later on 24 March, he drafted a *"Bericht über 160er E-Flugzeuge"* ("Report on the 160 [hp] E-Airplanes") in which he was critical of the climbing capability, maneuverability and engine power of the type. He also stated that "the mounting of the machine guns at an elevation of fifteen degrees is unsatisfactory."[38] After complaining that it made aiming more difficult and wasted ammunition, he noted: *"Der Unterschied ist mir gerade jetzt aufgefallen, wo ich zur Aushilfe wieder einen 100er fliege."* ("The difference is especially noticeable to me now that I am temporarily flying a 100 [type] again.")[39] The reference to elevated machine guns has confounded aero historians because none of the photos of Boelcke's E.IVs show such an arrangement. Perhaps the "new machine" Boelcke expected to get soon after 16 March was an E.IV that had elevated guns.[40] He may have tried it, found it quite unsatisfactory and abandoned it (at least until the guns had been readjusted to his liking). In any event, Boelcke temporarily switched back to a 100 hp E.II or E.III, which means that 123/15 was not available at this time. This was probably due to the incident related by Franz Immelmann: "Once in March, 1916... the struts attaching the engine to the machine broke after one of Boelcke's flights, but he succeeded in landing."[41] Boelcke subsequently traveled to Schwerin to confer with Fokker a few days later, after which he went home to Dessau for a short visit. During this period at Sivry, he managed to add four more to his score to bring his total to 13.

Fokker D.III prototype (later 350/16)
(sometime between 26 March and 7 April 1916)
While at Schwerin, Fokker had Boelcke try out his D.III (M 19) prototype. It employed the same 160 hp Oberursel U.III twin-row rotary engine that powered the E.IV but in a more modern biplane design. A famous postcard (B21) featured Boelcke in the cockpit of this unarmed plane.[42] For more photographs of the prototype both before and after its acceptance by the military (where it was then assigned the serial number 350/16), see Grosz, *Fokker Fighters D.I–IV*, pp.29–31.

Fokker E.IV 123/15
(mid-December 1915 – June 1916) - continued
Boelcke returned to the Front around 11 April 1916. Tragedy struck ten days later when his partner, *Lt.* Werner Notzke, was killed in a flying accident on 21 April. Returning from a fight in which he had experienced a machine gun jam, Notzke flew to a spot near Sivry field to test-fire the gun. On his third pass, his wing struck the cable of a balloon tethered nearby (that morning was the first time it had been raised there) which sent him crashing to the ground. *Oblt.* Ernst von Althaus was one of two replacement pilots brought in the next week. B22 is a photo of Boelcke and Althaus at Sivry field in front of 123/15, which now shows signs of more advanced

B21: A postcard showing Boelcke in the cockpit of Fokker's unarmed D.III prototype.

B22: Boelcke (in flight gear) and *Oblt*. Ernst von Althaus (far right) have a conversation in front of 123/15. The white band and rudder are more heavily stained than seen in the previous photos. Incidentally, the mechanic standing just left of Boelcke is the same man who appears at far right in B20.

B23–24: Two more snapshots of 123/15 in a more weathered condition. The first comes from a set of pictures that featured Boelcke's E.IV in front of a lineup of biplanes. The second captures it just in front of either an E.II or E.III that appears to be the same one as in B18.

weathering – particularly on the rudder and underneath the cross pattée on the fuselage's white band. The paint on the wheels appears to have dulled as well. 123/15 has a similar appearance in B23–24. B25 shows Boelcke in an even more worn out 123/15: the white band is now heavily stained and paint has chipped off the tri-color wheel. Boelcke was at the Front, bringing his total up to 18, until late on 21 May when he departed on an extended home leave.

It was probably sometime during this period that the E.IV that eventually bore the six-pointed star symbol on its wheel (B10–11) was delivered to Boelcke. B26 has Boelcke in the cockpit of this plane – we know this because the stylized "OB" symbol on its cowling is an exact match as is the rarely-seen, small sight mounted on the starboard machine gun (despite the port gun having the more traditional rectangular sight). Peter Grosz's study of the E.IV model mentions that the bump seen on this E.IV's turtledeck just forward of the cockpit was characteristic of later production machines.[43] The photos Grosz published show the bump on E.IV 641/15, which came late in the third production batch (serial numbers 637–642/15) and all the E.IVs from the last batch (serial numbers 160–189/16). These planes were delivered to the Front from late March through August 1916.[44] B26's E.IV is heavily stained and weathered, indicating that it had been in use for some time. Boelcke's last flight in an E.IV occurred on 28 June, so this plane was likely delivered several months before that. It is just possible that it was the "new machine" Boelcke mentioned on 16 March – a notion supported by the special "OB" symbol attached to its cowling; however, without more evidence, this remains purely speculative.

Boelcke started out for the Front again on 2 June 1916 and probably arrived back at Sivry the next day. He wrote on the 12th that there was not much going on. A few days later, however, a German plane that had been harassed by a Nieuport landed at Sivry. The crew informed Boelcke that six planes bearing the American flag on their fuselages were aloft and that one had attacked them. Boelcke related: "Well, I did not think it was quite so bad as all that and took off to say how-do-you-do to the six 'Americans' – that was the least they could expect, and courtesy required it of me... I was using my machine for the first time after it had come back from the factory and got jams after twenty shots with the left gun and fifty with the right one."[45] Thus it appears that either Boelcke's 123/15 or the spare E.IV seen in B26 had been sent back to Fokker's Schwerin factory for refurbishment during Boelcke's leave and had only just returned in mid-June.

Halbersdtadt D.II
(sometime during 22–26 June 1916)
Shortly after Immelmann's death on 18 June, Boelcke flew 123/15 (or the other E.IV seen in B26) over to Douai for the memorial ceremony. He stayed awhile at Douai and flew several combat

B25 Blowup above.

B25: Boelcke preparing to fire up the engine of 123/15. It is decidely more weathered in this snapshot, with more noticeable staining on the white band. The same "OB" insignia visible in B20 is just discernible on the cowling.

B26: This is Boelcke's other E.IV. Note the symmetrical guns, more cut-back cowling, bump on the turtledeck forward of the cockpit and different metal side panel affixed to the fuselage (it curves back rather than drops straight down) – these are all features of later production models. The "OB" initials presented in the blowup tell us that this was the same plane photographed in B10–11; however, it is heavily stained and does not yet have a six-pointed star symbol painted on its wheel covers. **B26 Blowup** inset.

missions there in his E.IV.[46] He also made a combat flight in one of the earliest Halberstadt D.II (or D.III) fighters that had originally been intended for Immelmann. It had arrived at Douai on 22 June, the day of Immelmann's memorial service. B27, which has *Oblt*. Ernst von Althaus and Boelcke standing next to new Halberstadt fighter, may be a photo of that plane. Althaus is not wearing the *Pour le Mérite* he was awarded on 21 July 1916, so we know the picture was taken before that event. Boelcke departed from the Front at the end of June for his tour of the Eastern Front, so this narrows down the

B27: *Oblt.* Ernst von Althaus (second from left), *Lt.* Alfred Lenz (third from left), Oswald Boelcke and *Lt.* Dietsch stand close to a pristine-looking Halbersatdt D.II. This may have been the early model delivered to Douai just a few days after Immelmann's death that Boelcke test flew and took into combat after attending Immelmann's memorial service.

timing even further. Peter Grosz tells us that the "first eight Halberstadt D.II and D.III fighters came to the Front in June 1916..."[47] Therefore, this photo must have been snapped in June 1916 when Boelcke noted that he flew one for the first time at Douai.

Roland C.II
(1916) (see p.31 for photo)

Fokker E.IV 123/15
(mid-December 1915 – June 1916) - continued
Boelcke was then summoned to meet with the Chief of the Air Service, *Oberstleutnant* Hermann Thomsen, at Charleville where he learned on 27 June that he was not to fly any more for the time being. Nevertheless, he flew two more missions that evening and was successful in one, bringing his tally up to 19. He went up again the next day, but this time it was only to visit with and say goodbye to brother Wilhelm before going on his enforced tour of the Eastern Front. And that, as far as we know, was Boelcke's final flight in a Fokker E.IV.

So where does this leave his two E.IVs as seen in B10? Boelcke was told in June 1916 that he was to lead a *Staffel* composed solely of Fokkers but was sent away from the Front just one day before its official formation on 30 June 1916. The unit went on without him and was integrated with *Fokkerstaffel* Jametz to create *Fokkerstaffel* Sivry, which counted men such as Hans Gutermuth, Ernst Hess, Fritz Loerzer and Friedrich Mallinckrodt among its ranks. On 25 August, *Fokkerstaffel* Sivry formed the basis of the newly-founded *Jasta* 6. B10 shows both 123/15 and Boelcke's spare E.IV in very clean condition. 123/15 is almost immaculate in its appearance (i.e., there is no staining, and the serial number and even the lifting instructions stenciled along the bottom longeron are clearly legible), no longer sports the white band/tri-color wheels scheme it once had and has a new turtle deck that displays the bump forward of the cockpit that was employed on later production models. The spare E.IV shows minor staining along the bottom of the fuselage and now bears a relatively unmarked six-pointed star symbol on its wheel. Clearly, both planes had recently been refurbished. Boelcke mentioned that one of them had just returned from the factory in mid-June, and his personal communications indicate that he only used it sparingly before he was temporarily banned from further combat flying. Judging from its minor signs of use, this could have been his spare E.IV. The one numbered 123/15 may have been overhauled after the spare had been returned – hence its immaculate condition in B10. Whatever the case, we

B28: A closeup portrait of Oswald Boelcke in E.IV 123/15.

B29: These snapshots, taken from a stereoscopic photo collection, depict Boelcke on duty in front of a Fokker E.III (428/15) identified as "*seinem Fokker*" ("his Fokker"). The only records we have of him using an E.III on the Western Front come from his time at *B.A.M.* (late September through early December 1915) and possibly when he temporarily switched to a 100 hp type in March 1916. The aircraft pictured could be of one of them.

can now be fairly certain that B10 captured Boelcke's two E.IVs sometime in July or early August 1916 after their master had been forced to leave them behind.

Boelcke was not finished with the Fokker *Eindecker*, however. Emil Meinecke recalled that when Boelcke visited Ottoman *FFA* 6 at Chanak-Kale in the Dardanelles on 28–30 July 1916: "Since *Oberleutnant* Croneiss was not present, *Hauptmann* Boelcke and I flew together, each in a Fokker E.III, and made reconnaissance flights over the islands of Imbros, Tenedos, and Mitylene… these islands were occupied by the English and they had their flying fields there. We flew every day as long as *Hauptmann* Boelcke was with us; however, we

B30–31: Oswald Boelcke's Fokker D.III 352/16 after it had been spruced up for museum display and as it appeared in Berlin's Zeughaus museum. The photos below tell us that the paint applied to the cowling, metal panels aft of the cowling and upper wing surfaces were not original to Boelcke's time.

did not see a single Englishman in the air."[48] One wonders what Boelcke's superiors would have had to say if he had encountered the enemy and shot one down while still under the Kaiser's ban from combat flying!

Fokker D.III 352/16
(2–16 September 1916)
Jasta 2 was formed on 27 August 1916 with Oswald Boelcke as its commander. During the first few days of its existence, the unit had no aircraft. Then Boelcke reported on 4 September: "Several days ago Fokker sent two machines for me, and I made my first flight on one of them the day before yesterday."[49] Prof. Werner identified one as 352/16, which was later presented to Berlin's Zeughaus museum and displayed there (B30–31).[50] Three shots of Boelcke and 352/16 (B32–34) were taken together at *Jasta* 2's Vélu airfield some time before Boelcke switched over to his new Albatros D.II fighter on 17 September. During this brief period, Boelcke downed seven more planes (five of them in one week) to raise his total to 26.

Albatros D.I
(on occasion during 2–16 September 1916)
On 17 September, Boelcke informed his parents: "The *Staffel* is not quite up to strength yet, as I am still without about half of our machines. But yesterday at least six arrived, so that I shall be able to take off with my *Staffel* for the first time today. Hitherto I have generally flown Fokker biplanes, but today I shall take up one of the new

B32–34: Boelcke and 352/16 at Vélu field before he moved on to his new Albatros. Considering that Boelcke only flew this plane for two weeks, it evidently did not take very long for its castor oil lubricant and exhaust to begin soiling the fuselage.

Albatroses."[51] Boelcke's qualifier, "generally" ("*meist*" in the original German), discloses that he did not confine himself to the two Fokkers sent his way. We are aware of only one other plane on *Jasta* 2's roster during this period, and it was the Albatros

B35: Fokker's D.III prototype, 350/16, after its acceptance into military service (see page 3 for another view of the plane). Boelcke's 352/16 looked quite similar.

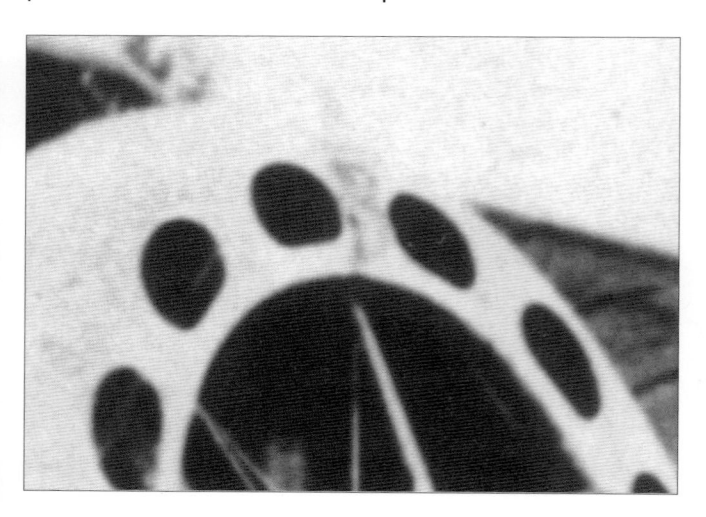

B36 & B36 blowup (above): Boelcke's Fokker D.III 352/16 at Vélu airfield. Though its cowling might have borne both his initials like his Fokker E.IVs, only a stylized 'B' is discernible here.

D.I brought over by *Fw.* Leopold Rudolf Reimann from *Jasta* 1 on 1 September after he had been reassigned to Boelcke's unit.

Albatros D.II 386/16
(17 September – 28 October 1916)
On 16 September, Boelcke and his pilots went to *Armee-Flug-Park* 1 to collect five Albatros D.Is and Boelcke's D.II 386/16. As related above, Boelcke took his new Albatros up the next day. He never looked back and put both men and machines through their paces. Boelcke summarized: "You will be interested to know that the official report of our activities which I have drawn up for the *Staffel's* September work includes one hundred and eighty-six front flights, in the course of which sixty-nine fights took place and twenty-five victories were

B36A: Submitted just before this volume went to press, here is a rare photograph of Boelcke's Fokker D.III 352/16 in front of one of *Jasta* 2's tents. Lubricant stains are visible on the fuselage side near the cockpit.

B36B: Another late submission is shown below. This is the Albatros D.II prototype at Johannisthal airfield. Aero historians James Miller and Greg VanWyngarden have identified multiple matching attributes between it and Oswald Boelcke's 386/16, including the small, rectangular plate attached to the fuselage just behind the cockpit. Extensive research has failed to discover any other D.II bearing such a plate, so they were almost certainly the same plane. Thus we see 386/16 here before its machine guns were fitted, windscreen changed, and serial number applied to the fin. (A small tube just under the cockpit's port side coaming through which signal flares were fired was also subsequently added, but this was probably done in the field.) Note the mottled paint effect on the rudder and lower left wing.

B37–42: This series of pictures occurred shortly after Oswald Boelcke had brought down his 34th victim on 16 October 1916. Boelcke had tangled with DH.2s from RFC No.24 Squadron and shot down A2542, piloted by Lt. P.A. Langan-Byrne (who was killed). The first photo is a closeup of Boelcke in D.II 386/16 after he had landed the plane at Lagnicourt field and parked it. A ground crewman waits near the tail for Boelcke to disembark. The second shows Boelcke exiting the plane as a gaggle of *Jasta* 2 airmen await him. The only men who can be identified for certain here are *Lt*. Hans Imelmann (second from left, hand in pocket), *Lt*. Hans Wortmann (fourth from left, head slightly turned with glasses), *Lt*. Erich König (sixth from left, light hat band and swagger stick), Boelcke and his crewman (underneath Boelcke next to plane). Some historians have placed *Lt*. Manfred von Richthofen and *Lt*. Erwin Böhme at first and third from the left (or vice versa), but this cannot be confirmed. The third snapshot has Boelcke's crewman helping in unwrapping his scarf as König smokes a cigarette at right. The fourth has Boelcke on the ground in his flight coat with his crewman behind him. Note the gloves resting on the fuselage just forward of the horizontal stabilizer. The men who can be identified here are König (second from left, light hat band), *Oblt*. Stefan Kirmaier (fifth from the right), Boelcke and his crewman. In the fifth and sixth scenes, Boelcke has removed his flight coat and begins to wipe machine gun powder stains from his face. König (fifth from the left, light hat band), Kirmaier (next to him, now bare-headed) and Imelmann (next to Kirmaier with hand in pocket) can be identified in the fifth, with the same going for Wortmann (second from left with glasses) and König (fourth from left, light hat band) in the sixth.

B41

won. This in spite of the fact that we did not really begin operations until our machines arrived on the 16th."[52] Boelcke continued to fly 386/16 until his death in it on 28 October 1916. During this period, he racked up his final 14 victories to close his total at 40.

B42

B43

B44

B43–44: When discussing the talismans and superstitions of airmen, Lothar von Richthofen related: *"Sich vor einem Start an der Front photographieren zu lassen, bringt Unglück. So ist Boelcke einmal vor dem Start photographiert worden. Von diesem Fluge kehrte er dann nicht zurück."* (Richthofen, *Ein Heldenleben*, p.222) ("It is unlucky to allow oneself to be photographed before taking off at the Front. Boelcke was once photographed this way before takeoff. He did not return from that flight.") These two snapshots have been cited as the sources of that belief. In the first, a ground crewman helps Boelcke don the last of his flight apparel. The second captures Boelcke, now in full flight gear, posing in front of D.II 386/16 while its engine runs prior to takeoff. Note the flight leader streamer blowing back from the lower wing behind the national insignia. This second photo first appeared in an article written about a visit with Boelcke the day of his death (see p.26 above) and therefore may well have been the last picture taken of him alive.

End Notes

[1] Werner, *Boelcke: der Mensch*, p.53; *Knight of Germany*, p.53.

[2] The exact nature and timing of the firm's transition is difficult to determine today. Some sources relate that Deutsche Bristol-Werke took over another company named "Halberstädter Flugplatzgesellschaft" and subsequently renamed itself "Halberstädter Flugzeugwerke GmbH" either in July 1913 or September 1914. In any event, the British Bristol company continued to keep partial ownership in the venture until the advent of World War I forced its interests to be divested, like so many other international partnerships of the day. Boelcke went from referring to the aircraft as "Bristol-*Taubes*" in a 16 June 1914 letter, to "*Taubes*" on 3 July and then "Halberstadt *Taubes*" from 14 July forward.

[3] *Boelcke: der Mensch*, p.57; *Knight of Germany*, p.58.

[4] *Boelcke: der Mensch*, p.58; *Knight of Germany*, p.59.

[5] They mostly flew with one another as well, as confirmed by Boelcke's 26 March 1915 letter: "...not so long ago the chief wanted to separate us brothers who have flown together so successfully for six months..." (*Knight of Germany*, p.84; *Boelcke: der Mensch*, p.79)

[6] *Boelcke: der Mensch*, pp.69–70; *Knight of Germany*, pp.72–73 (which misdates the letter as "5.10.14" instead of the original's "25.10.14").

[7] *Boelcke: der Mensch* had "*Eindecker*" here but *Knight of Germany* mistakenly translated it as "biplane." In addition, a portion of the original German passage – relating that Parschau "*jetzt bei einer Nachbarabteilung*" ("now at a neighboring *Abteilung*") – was omitted in the English translation.

[8] *Knight of Germany*, pp.79–80; *Boelcke: der Mensch*, pp.75–76. Initial production models of the A.I/M.8 were delivered in October 1914 and *Lt.* Otto Parschau, who had used one of Fokker's early M.5 aircraft and thereby gotten to know the designer, was among the first to get one.

[9] A distinguishing characteristic of the A.I/M.8 was that the aft, inboard sections of the wings were not attached to the fuselage, which is evident in the photo.

[10] *Knight of Germany*, p.101; *Boelcke: der Mensch*, p.94.

[11] *Knight of Germany*, p.114; *Boelcke: der Mensch*, p.105.

[12] *Eagle of Lille*, pp.103–04; *Adler von Lille*, pp.91–92.

[13] *Eagle of Lille*, p.105; *Adler von Lille*, p.93.

[14] "Als Beobachter Boelckes im Westen," p.217. *FFA* 62's CO, *Hptm.* Hermann Kastner, had distinguished himself flying a Fokker M.5L spotter with *FFA* 38 in Belgium and later on the Eastern Front, so he was well-known to Fokker. Parschau knew Boelcke from their time together in Darmstadt and had been the one to inspire Boelcke to obtain his A.I/M.8 artillery spotter at *FFA* 13. We can infer from all this that the choice of *FFA* 62's airfield for their demonstration flights was more than mere happenstance.

[15] *Knight of Germany*, pp.106–07; *Boelcke: der Mensch*, p.99.

[16] *Knight of Germany*, p.108; *Boelcke: der Mensch*, p.100.

[17] On 28 July 1915, Parschau wrote: "As of 16 July, I departed from *Abteilung* 62 and am now again at *BAO* in Ghistelles..The five aircraft that were delivered to Douai with the MG 08 have proven to be excellent. My students there have not experienced a jam up to now. Yesterday, I was in Lille at Freyburg's *Abteilung*, and there an *offizierstellvertreter* had a combat during which 540 rounds were fired without stoppage." (VanWyngarden, *Early German Aces of World War I*, p.10) *FFA* 5 and 24 were based near Lille at this time.

[18] For example, his 3 August 1915 letter says "The next day I had a trial in one of the two war machines." (*Eagle of Lille*, p.116; *Adler von Lille*, p.102) and his 11 September letter states "All sections here have a Fokker. We are the only one with two." (*Eagle of Lille*, p.131; *Adler von Lille*, p.114)

[19] *Knight of Germany*, pp.107, 118; *Boelcke: der Mensch*, pp.99, 109.

[20] We know of at least one occasion where Boelcke returned to what was probably C.I 162/15. One of his letters mentioned that after he was summoned to visit with Prince Aribert of Anhalt at the Front on 21 August 1915, "I took him up in my biplane in the afternoon – my Fokker is too narrow to contain such big men..." (*Knight of Germany*, p.120; *Boelcke: der Mensch*, p.111) Boelcke also mentions in a 22 September 1915 letter that due to the long distance of some reconnaissance missions, he occasionally had to revert to a biplane because of its greater range.

Wühlisch continued to accompany him on such flights until he was wounded in August. Thereafter Boelcke took Ehrhardt von Teubern along.

[21] *Eagle of Lille*, p.181; *Adler von Lille*, p.157.
[22] Despite one photo's claim in *Knight of Germany/Boelcke: der Mensch* that it is of "The E.3; Boelcke's first Fokker single-seater," we know that it actually shows the first E.II that Anthony Fokker demonstrated before Crown Prince Wilhelm at Stenay on 13 June 1915 (e.g., see Grosz, *Fokker E.I/II*, pp.10–11).
[23] *Adler von Lille*, p.102; *Eagle of Lille*, p.116 (which translated "*Übungsmaschine*" as "school machine."
[24] *Boelcke: der Mensch*, p.113; *Knight of Germany*, pp.122–23, had a slightly different translation than the one given here and also misdated the letter as "9.8.15" instead of "9.9.15."
[25] *Eagle of Lille*, p.138; *Adler von Lille*, p.120. Immelmann was catching his family up on September events in a letter dated 11 October 1915.
[26] *Knight of Germany*, p.127; *Boelcke: der Mensch*, p.117
[27] *Knight of Germany*, p.131; *Boelcke: der Mensch*, p.121. Teubern had also been transferred to *B.A.M.* and accompanied Boelcke during his occasional biplane excursions while he awaited the arrival of his new Fokker *Eindecker*.
[28] *Knight of Germany*, pp.135; *Boelcke: der Mensch*, pp.125.
[29] *Adler von Lille*, p.138; *Eagle of Lille*, p.160, which uses a slightly different translation.
[30] E.IV serial numbers were 122–127/15, 436–441/15, 637–642/15, 160–89/16 and LF.210 (navy).
[31] The offset machine guns are believed to have been the result of the first few E.IVs having been originally constructed to accomodate three guns: one to port, one to starboard and the last in between. Fokker ran into problems with synchronizing them, however, so one (port side) was removed before actual delivery. Photo evidence tells us that Parschau's 122/15, Boelcke's 123/15, and Wintgens' 124/15 all had offset machine guns. By the time Immelmann's 127/15 was produced, the guns were centered on the nose. 122/15 and 123/15 also displayed the fuller, pug-nosed cowling, whereas 124/15 and beyond did not.
[32] It was once suggested that the "OB" might have stood for Oberursel, the engine manufacturer; but after examining numerous contemporaneous newspaper and magazine advertisements for that company, this writer has found absolutely no support for this notion. Moreover, no "OB" markings are evident among the many other extant Fokker *Eindecker* photos unconnected to Boelcke. The only similar example we have is when we see Anthony Fokker's initials, "AF," affixed to the same spot on the cowling of E.IV 122/15

– the first of the line that he used for demonstrations before handing it over to Otto Parschau.
[33] See Grosz, *Fokker E.IV*, p.5.
[34] *Knight of Germany*, p.137; *Boelcke: der Mensch*, p.127.
[35] *Knight of Germany*, p.149; *Boelcke: der Mensch*, p.137.
[36] Ibid.
[37] *Knight of Germany*, p.155; *Boelcke: der Mensch*, p.142.
[38] *Knight of Germany*, p.160; *Boelcke: der Mensch*, p.147.
[39] *Boelcke: der Mensch*, p.148. *Knight of Germany*, p.160 omits "temporarily."
[40] The only photos of an E.IV with elevated guns are of the prototype, eventually designated E.IV 122/15. At first, it sported three machine guns; later, it carried only two. We know this machine was at first delivered to *Lt*. Otto Parschau in late 1915 for evaluation and probable operational use, but its history after that is uncertain. It is possible – though purely speculative – that Fokker reclaimed it and delivered it to Boelcke for his evaluation in March 1916.
[41] *Eagle of Lille*, p.91; *Adler von Lille*, p.81.
[42] For a detailed discussion of the postcard and when its picture originated, see Bronnenkant, *Imperial German Eagles 3*, pp.261–64.
[43] Grosz, *Fokker E.IV*, p.4.
[44] Ibid., p.9.
[45] *Knight of Germany*, pp.176–77; *Boelcke: der Mensch*, p.162.
[46] We know he took an E.IV on his trip because while describing the events taking place there, he made statements like "I took off with the other Fokkers from Douai. As I had the fastest machine...," "I could not quite finish him off because my left gun jammed when I had shot away all the ammunition in my right.," and "I saw another 160 h.p. machine..." (*Knight of Germany*, p.179; *Boelcke: der Mensch*, p.164)
[47] *Halberstadt Fighters*, p.5.
[48] *Cross & Cockade* 12:3, p.240.
[49] *Knight of Germany*, p.205; *Boelcke: der Mensch*, p.186.
[50] The other Fokker may have been D.I 185/16. A photo from Erwin Böhme's personal album (see *Over the Front* 8:4, p.296) has him posing in front of this plane "at Bertincourt." *Jasta* 2 left Bertincourt on the evening of 22 September, by which time the unit had already begun using its Albatros fighters.
[51] *Knight of Germany*, p.209; *Boelcke: der Mensch*, pp.189–90.
[52] *Knight of Germany*, p.215; *Boelcke: der Mensch*, p.195.

Above: Oswald Boelcke was featured on many German postcards in 1916, even though he personally disliked such publicity and attention. Here are three of them issued by the prolific postcard manufacturer, Neue Photographische Gesellschaft (NPG). This private enterprise was at the forefront of its industry and developed the basic technology for color photography and light-sensitive paper that was later used for decades. The first two NPG cards were issued while Boelcke was alive; the last one was a posthumous offering. All three featured images of Boelcke that had been taken by court photographer Julius Müller when Boelcke was home on a late-May through early June 1916 leave in Dessau.

Above: This recently discovered picture captures Boelcke's four mechanics (seen in B20 on p.43) attending Fokker E.IV 123/15 at Sivry. (photo courtesy of Charles G. Thomas)

Boelcke – Military Service

Significant Dates

19 May 1891	born in Giebichenstein (near Halle)
15 Mar 1911	admitted into army as *Fahnenjunker*
31 Jul 1912	certified as an *Offizier/Degenfähnrich*
18 Aug 1912	certified as a *Leutnant* (but Officer's Patent antedated to 23 August 1910)
Jun 1914	began flight training at Halberstadt
3 Jul 1914	first solo flight
13 Jul 1914	passed Pilot's Exam 1
31 Jul 1914	passed Pilot's Exam 2
15 Aug 1914	passed Pilot's Exam 3
1 Sep 1914	assigned to *Feldflieger-Abteilung* 13
8 Dec 1914	flew first Fokker monoplane (type A.I/M.8)
26 Apr 1915	assigned to *Feldflieger-Abteilung* 62
4 Jul 1915	first victory (in LVG C.I biplane)
19 Sep 1915	assigned to *Brieftauben-Abteilung Metz*
11 Dec 1915	back at *Feldflieger-Abteilung* 62
12 Jan 1916	awarded *Pour le Mérite*
21 Jan 1916	assigned to *Artillerie-Flieger-Abteilung* 203
27 Jan 1916	promoted to *Oberleutnant*
11 Mar 1916	headed independent *Fokkerstaffel* at Sivry
21 May 1916	promoted to *Hauptmann*
8 Jul 1916	began tour of Balkans, Turkey, Eastern Front
20 Aug 1916	returned home to Dessau
27 Aug 1916	*Jasta* 2 first assembled at Vélu
26 Oct 1916	final victory (#40)
28 Oct 1916	killed in midair collision
31 Oct 1916	memorial service in Cambrai
2 Nov 1916	buried in Dessau

Service Units

15 Mar 191–29 May 1914	*Telegraphen-Bataillon* Nr.3 (technically, Boelcke remained a member throughout his aviation career)
1 Jun 191–early Aug 1914	Halberstadt Flight School
Remainder Aug 1914	*Flieger-Ersatz-Abteilung* 3
1 Sep 1914–25 Apr 1915	*Feldflieger-Abteilung* 13
26 Apr 1915–18 Sep 1915	*Feldflieger-Abteilung* 62
19 Sep 1915–10 Dec 1915	*Brieftauben-Abteilung Metz*
11 Dec 1915–21 Jan 1916	*Feldflieger-Abteilung* 62
22 Jan 1916–10 Mar 1916	Fokker detachment of *Artillerie-Flieger-Abteilung* 203 at Jametz
11 Mar 1916–30 Jun 1916	*Fokkerstaffel* at Sivry
27 Aug 1916–28 Oct 1916	*Jagdstaffel* 2

Awards

15 Aug 1914	Pilot's Badge – Germany
12 Oct 1914	Iron Cross, 2nd Class – Prussia
27 Jan 1915	Iron Cross, 1st Class – Prussia
31 Jan 1915	Friedrich Cross, 2nd Class – Anhalt
3 Nov 1915	Royal Hohenzollern House Order, Knight's Cross with Swords – Prussia*
8 Nov 1915	House Order of Albert the Bear, Knight's Cross 2nd Class with Swords – Anhalt
13 Nov 1915	Military Merit Order, 4th Class with Swords – Bavaria
30 Nov 1915	Life Saving Medal – Prussia
25 Dec 1915	*Ehrenbecher* – Germany
12 Jan 1916	*Pour le Mérite* – Prussia
15 Jul 1916	War Medal – Ottoman Empire**
15–20 Jul 1916	Pilot's Badge – Ottoman Empire***
31 Jul 1916	Saxe-Ernestine House Order, Knight 1st Class with Swords – Saxon Duchies
9 Aug 1916	Bravery Order, 4th Class, 2nd Degree – Bulgaria
19 Sep 1916	Military Merit Order, Knight – Württemberg
25 Oct 1916	Order of the Iron Crown, 3rd Class with War Decoration – Austria-Hungary
Unknown	House Order of Albert the Bear, Knight's Cross 1st Class with Swords – Anhalt
Unknown	Imtiaz Medal in Silver – Ottoman Empire (likely 23 Jul 1916)

*Notified of award on 1 Nov.; document dated 3 Nov
**given award by Enver Pascha 15 July; document dated 23 Jul
***Boelcke wearing it in photo taken 20 Jul 1916

Above: The front and back of Prussia's Life Saving Medal. The ribbon is bright yellow with white side stripes.

Boelcke – Victory List

No.	Date	Aircraft	Location, Unit & Crew*
1	4 Jul 1915	Morane Parasol	near Marchiennes – Esc MS15: *Lt.* Maurice Têtu, *Lt.* Georges de la Rochefoucauld (b-KIA)
2	19 Aug	Bristol biplane	near Arras – RFC 2: *Cpt.* JG Hearson, *Cpt.* Barker (b-OK/ftl)
3	10 Sep	Nieuport 10	east Ablain-Saint-Nazaire – N15: *Cpt.* René Turin (WIA)
4	24 Sep	Voisin	near Pont-à-Mousson – VB103: *Sous-Lt.* Rodolphe Bordas, *Asp.* Renaud (b-OK)
5	16 Oct	Voisin V839	Saint-Souplet – VB110: *Cpl.* Gaston Vibert, *Sgt.* Robert Cadet (b-KIA)
6	30 Oct	Farman	near Sommepy-Tahure – MF8: *Lt.* Albert Dullin, *Lt.* Gaston Leclerc (b-KIA)
7	5 Jan 1916	BE.2c 1734	Harnes – RFC 2: 2Lt. William E Somervell, Lt. Geoffrey C Formilli (b-WIA/POW)
8	12 Jan	RE.7 2287	Mouscron – RFC 12: 2Lt. Leonard Kingdon (KIA), Lt. KW Gray (WIA/POW)
9	14 Jan	BE.2c 4087	near Bécourt – RFC 8: 2Lt. JH Herring, Cpt. R Erskine (b-WIA)
10	12 Mar	Farman	near Marre – Esc MF63: *MdL.* Jean Cellière, *Sous-Lt.* Jacques Loviconi (b-WIA)
11	13 Mar	Voisin	near Malancourt – ?
12	19 Mar	Farman	near Cuisy – Esc MF19: *Sgt.* Pierre Galiment, *Lt.* Jacques Libman (b-KIA)
13	21 Mar	Voisin V1417	near Fosses Wood – VB109: *Lt.* Jean Antonioli, *Cpt.* Félix Le Croart (b-KIA)
14	27 Apr	Farman	near Vaux – ?
15	1 May	French biplane	near Vaux – ?
16	18 May	Caudron	near Rouvroy-Ripont – Esc C56: *MdL.* Hubert Cagninacci, *S-Lt.* Louis Vivien (b-KIA)
17	21 May	Nieuport	near Mort Homme – Esc N65: *Adj.* Henri Brion (WIA)
18	" "	Nieuport	Bois-de-Hesse – Esc N65: *Sgt.* Georges Kirsch (WIA)
19	27 Jun	Nieuport	near Douaumont – ?
20	2 Sep	DH.2 7895	near Thiepval – RFC 32: Cpt. Robert E Wilson (POW)
21	8 Sep	FE.2b 4921	near Le Sars – RFC 22: Lt. EGA Bowen, Lt. RM Stalker (b-KIA)
22	9 Sep	DH.2 7842	near Bapaume – RFC 24: Lt. NP Manfield (KIA)
23	14 Sep	Sopwith Str A1910	near Morval – RFC 70: 2Lt. JH Gale, Spr. JM Strathy (b-KIA)
24	" "	DH.2 7873	Driencourt – RFC 24: 2Lt. JV Bowring (WIA/POW)
25	15 Sep	Sopwith Str A1910	near Hesbécourt – RFC 70: 2Lt. FH Bowyer (WIA/POW), 2Lt. WB Saint (DOW)
26	" "	Sopwith Str	near Èterpigny – ?
27	17 Sep	FE.2b 7019	Equancourt – RFC 11: Cpt. DB Gray, Lt. LB Helder (b-POW)
28	19 Sep	Morane V A204	Grévillers Wood – RFC 60: Cpt. HC Tower (KIA)
29	27 Sep	Martinsyde G102 A1568	near Ervillers – RFC 27: 2Lt. HA Taylor (KIA)
30	1 Oct	DH.2 A2533	near Flers – RFC 32: Cpt. HWG Jones (OK/ftl)
31	7 Oct	Nieuport 12	near Morval – ?
32	10 Oct	FE.2b 6992	near Pozières – RFC 11: Sgt. E Haxton, Cpl. BGF Jeffs (b-KIA)
33	16 Oct	BE.2d 6745	near Hébuterne – RFC 15: Sgt. F Barton, Lt. EM Carre (b-KIA)
34	" "	DH.2 A2542	near Beaulencourt – RFC 24: Lt. PAL Byrne (KIA)
35	17 Oct	FE.2b 6965	near Bullecourt – RFC 11: 2Lt. CL Roberts (POW), 2Lt. JL Pulleyn (KIA)
36	20 Oct	FE.2b 7674	near Agny – RFC 11: Lt. RP Harvey (WIA), 2Lt. GK Welsford (KIA)
37	22 Oct	Sopwith Str 7777	near Grévillers Wood – RFC 45: Cpt. L Porter (POW/DOW), 2Lt. GB Samuels (KIA)
38	" "	BE.12 6654	near Grévillers – RFC 21: 2Lt. WT Wilcox (POW)
39	25 Oct	BE.2d 5831	Puisieux – RFC 7: 2Lt. W Fraser, 2Lt. J Collen (b-KIA)
40	26 Oct	BE.2d 5781	near Serre – RFC 5: 2Lt. Smith (WIA), Lt. JC Jervis (KIA)

*pilot listed first
b   both occupants   KIA   killed in action
DOW   died of wounds   POW   prisoner of war
ftl   forced to land   WIA   wounded in action

Note: The list above provides new material for the dates and identities of some of Boelcke's victories. The author plans to address them in an upcoming, more detailed biography of Oswald Boelcke.

Max Immelmann

Above: This photograph of Max Immelmann was taken right after he was awarded the *Orden Pour le Mérite*.

Immelmann – The Man
Youth

At the beginning of the month in which he died, Max Immelmann responded to a request for personal information from Berlin author Emil Malkowsky. He did so in a succinct document that will be referred to henceforth as the Immelmann Summary.[1] It began: "I am herewith gladly willing to provide you with some biographical information because, in my opinion, it won't hurt anything if mistakes – which are common concerning me – are eliminated in this manner. Since I don't know how informed you are about my life, I must begin with my birthday and parents. Father: Franz Immelmann, born in Stendal. Profession: Factory owner in Dresden (cardboard packaging manufacturer). Mother: née Grimmer, daughter of General of Military Justice Grimmer in Dresden." Franz August Immelmann, son of the district of Stendal's veterinary surgeon, went to Dresden where he met his wife, Gertrud Sedonie Grimmer, the daughter of a *Generalauditeur* – one of the army's chief law officers.

Immelmann Summary: "The name 'Immelmann' is connected with 'Imme'= bees. Our ancestors probably were bee breeders in the borderlands. The family coat-of-arms displays three flying bees. Myself: born 21 September 1890 in Dresden. I have an older sister and a younger brother." Max's siblings were sister Elfriede and brother Franz who would later author Max's postwar biography.[2]

Immelmann Summary: "I was taken in my early youth to the so-called 'Weinberg' (owned by my grandfather) in Loschwitz heights near Dresden. Because of my father's illness, we moved from one convalescent place to another. Twice to Meran in the Tirol. The last one was the White Stag in Dresden. My father died of tuberculosis there in 1897." Brother Franz explained that the "Weinberg" was an estate in the hills of Loschwitz that belonged to *Generalauditeur* Grimmer. Father Franz became ill in 1893 and the three children also suffered from various maladies, so the family traveled to several locations seeking remedies. They finally returned to Weisser Hirsch ("White Stag"), a neighborhood outside of Dresden, where Dr. Heinrich Lahmann had established a sanatorium known by the same name that specialized in naturopathic medicine.[3] The internationally-recognized institution was a strong proponent of vegetarian diets and the limited intake of table salt and alcohol. Its regimen apparently did much to help cure the three children, but unfortunately for Franz Sr., it could not overcome the tuberculosis he succumbed to in 1897.

Immelmann Summary: "Education began at The White Stag's Municipal School in 1897–99, then the 4th Citizen's School at Dresden-Neustadt in 1899–1900; then the Royal Secondary School at Dresden in 1900, the Martino Catharineum (old secondary school) at Brunswick in 1901–03 (on account of repetition two years in the fifth form of secondary school), then the Dresden Cadet Corps in 1905–11... Activity before the war: already a strong interest in machines during my youth. Initial intention: become a mechanical engineer. In the Cadet Corps was a very good mathematician, came off less well at languages... Much enjoyment with pure mathematical studies." The Immelmann family went to Brunswick for a few years to be with Max's

Above: Max Immelmann was born in this Dresden house on 21 September 1890.

Above: Max Immelmann's family and dog, Tyras, sometime after his death. Brother Franz, who Oswald Boelcke said bore a striking resemblance to Max, is at left. Sister Elfriede (right) and mother Gertrud (seated) are wearing mourning clothes.

Left: A newspaper advertisement for the Weisser Hirsch Sanatorium.

aunt, Elsa Boetzel. Franz recalled: "In the glorious, untroubled freedom of youth we two schoolboys roamed the mysterious corridors and vaults of the Boetzel family's wine cellars; in the summer we made the vast expanses of the Pawel Woods unsafe for pedestrians and in the winter we made a nuisance of ourselves to the skaters on the rinks of the Civic Pond and the small parade ground."[4] Franz may not have been exaggerating because he admits that after their return to Dresden in 1904, his own "wildness" led to his being sent to a boarding house, and grandfather Grimmer suggested that Max be enrolled in Dresden's Cadet School. Max entered the school on 23 April 1905 and we have this glimpse into his personality at the time from an acquaintance: "I was still in school and often spent holidays with my friend, who is Immelmann's cousin, and whose parents had an estate with a large garden near Dresden. I ran into him there on a daily basis. He was a cadet in residence at the time and sometimes rode his bicycle to Freital-Deuben on his off-duty afternoons. I can still picture him quite clearly, when he would suddenly drop in our midst in his blue uniform, always with a happy, carefree, merry smile on his bright boyish face. We would then rush together around the garden, climb on the fruit trees or compete against each other riding on swings... But what we really admired at the time were his cycling tricks. He performed the wildest things with the greatest daring. He would go

Above: Max Immelmann as a member of the Dresden Cadet Corps.

Right: Max Immelmann during his early military service.

backwards, always crawling between both wheels or doing a headstand in the saddle. The road in front of the house was hilly and rolling, but that didn't seem to bother him one bit. He tried and tested everything... And whenever he arrived, there was shrill, nonstop bell ringing, and before you could be on the lookout for him, he was there like lightning. It was the same when he rode away. He'd swing himself up onto his bicycle and go off at racing speed, causing the children playing peacefully in the street to shriek and run away and chickens and geese to flutter off. And when the ever-shrinking, fleeing dot of his blue tunic disappeared around the last corner, then Max and his bold acts would be the talk of the day – which would last for at least an hour or so."[5] This depiction of an exuberant, boisterous lad speaks volumes about what brother Franz later wrote: "It was certainly no easy matter for one so accustomed to freedom to adapt himself to the strict order and discipline of the cadet corps, especially as his instructor was often forced to curtail his leave by way of punishment."[6]

Immelmann spent the first two summers of his Cadet Corps years at Jungborn, the nature cure sanatorium founded by Adolf Just in the Harz mountains, which also advocated vegetarianism and the avoidance of alcohol and nicotine. Max adopted this philosophy and adhered to it for most of the rest of his life.[7] But it caused some probems for him with his schoolmates, who "chaffed him for his repugnance to any form of meat food and his dislike of alcohol." He also had no desire to become an officer because he did not "wish to be bound by the stiff etiquette of a particular caste."[8] Consequently, Immelmann contemplated leaving the Cadet Corps in 1908 to pursue a technical profession, but was convinced by his mother to stay the course. He eventually grew to become an exemplary cadet, as reported by his company commander: "By reason of his good character and qualities Immelmann is a very pleasant person with excellent manners. Home work – praiseworthy. He has proven himself completely as the senior soldier in the barracks; he goes to much trouble and looks after the younger cadets well. In practical service he is one of the best; his bearing is definite and full of assurance. Leadership – excellent."[9] His academic record showed a strong interest in the sciences, demonstrated by one of his last reports where he received a 1 or 1b grade (excellent) in Chemistry, Physics, Mathematics and Geometrical Drawing but only a 3 (sufficient) in languages (Latin, French, English). Immelmann also pursued various athletic activities. He took up gymnastics and became renowned at the school for his trick cycling and acrobatic displays; and he ascended several mountain peaks and went on a bicycle tour of Europe going from Dresden to Cologne, Brussels, Paris and Boppard during his final years with the corps. Before Immelmann graduated in March 1911, he had to make a choice concerning which type of army technical unit he would like to serve in as an officer. Though tempted by the Pioneers, he chose the railway troops.

Early Military Career

Immelmann Summary: "Entered Railway Regiment 2 as an officer candidate in 1911, then attended the War School at Anklam from August 1911 to March 1912. Returned to the regiment, requested time off to serve in the reserves and studied mechanical engineering at Dresden's Technical University from May 1912 to August 1914... Service with the Railway Regiment offered little satisfaction; therefore took up old plan: studied mechanical engineering. During student days took up sport activities: motorcycling and auto sports. Much enjoyment with pure mathematical studies." *Fahnenjunker* Max Immelmann arrived at *Eisenbahn-Regiment* Nr. 2's barracks at Schöneberg on 4 April 1911 only to find that no one expected him. They had somehow forgotten that they had accepted him among their ranks. This inauspicious start set the tone for his time there. He found that the officers had little practical engineering knowledge and therefore equally little to offer him from that standpoint. When he sought to learn from the men in the ranks, he was shunned by his superiors: "How can they

Above: This artist's rendering of Immelmann in front of one of his victories was drawn by *Bootsmannsmaat* (Boatswain's Mate) Richard Fiedler.

take it amiss because I respect the knowledge and the practical work of anyone, even though he is only a simple workman, and try to profit by it?"[10] His letters home demonstrate that he constantly vacillated between staying with the military or leaving to pursue an engineering degree. When he was posted to the War Academy at Anklam in early August 1911, his situation did not improve much: "Whenever I find any time, I read mathematical works. The study of military tactics, which are the basis of an officer's career, leave me completely cold. Tactics are mainly a matter of intuition, so that one can learn only their most general principles. I am always amazed at the way many ensigns here can say the right thing in questions of tactics at the first attempt, just as others are amazed when anyone's motor cycle will not work and I say at the first inspection: 'This or that is wrong.'"[11] Both to ease his boredom and satisfy his quest for practical technical knowledge, Immelmann had begun to tinker with motorcycles and automobiles. Self-taught through dismantling and reassembling them, he became quite mechanically adept. One other technical application seized his imagination at the end of one of the academy's instructional tours. In January 1912, he was taken to Johannisthal: "That was the crown of our tour of instruction. One seldom sees anything so splendid. They showed us all the most important machines, such as the Wrights, Rumplers and Farmans, explained their construction and demonstrated three of them. It was a glorious and unique sight when these aeroplanes, which resembled huge birds, soared into the air and executed daring turns and glides with a truly amazing self-confidence."[12] Immelmann finally decided to leave the military but wanted to complete his officer's examinations first. After learning that he had achieved a "good" in them, he turned in his resignation papers, which were accepted in mid-April 1912. He was now a *Degenfähnrich* (sword-knot ensign) in the reserves and could attend Dresden's Technical University.

Immelmann immersed himself in mechanical studies including a stint at nearby Reick's turbine factory. He purchased, worked on and then sold several motorized vehicles. He also vigorously pursued athletic activities, joining a gymnastics club, dancing, playing tennis and iceskating in the winter. Having remembered his experience at Johannisthal, he first joined the Technical Aviation Association, where he built model airplanes, and then the Air Fleet League, where he took part as an official in the flying competitions held at Caditz airfield in 1913–14. But then his life, along with the lives of millions of others around the world, was interrupted by the outbreak of World War I.

Airman

Immelmann Summary: "Called up to Railway Regiment 1 on 18 August 1914... Unwarlike building activity unsatisfactory... went to the aviation school at Johannisthal on 13 November 1914. Transferred to another in May... Good average student at flying school. Passed first and second examinations on 9 and 11 February; third examination on 26 March. Went to an *Abteilung* in the Champagne region at the beginning of April, then to another *Abteilung* in northern France in early May. First observation flights there. With Boelcke in the same *Abteilung*." When the world began to go to war in early August 1914, Immelmann disliked the prospect of doing his duty in a railway regiment. Accordingly, when he and his brother saw an *Idflieg* (Inspectorate of Aviation Troops) recruitment request for men with technical experience on 10 August, Max immediately filed a transfer application.[13] While awaiting the results, he was called up into *Eisenbahn-Regiment* Nr.1 on 20 August.[14] There,

Above: Max Immelmann (right) and Erhardt von Teubern soon after their Iron Cross, 2nd Class awards (seen here dangling from the front of their tunics) were bestowed upon them.

while watching others march off to what then was believed to be the glory of war, he spent his time near Berlin on garrison duty. His frustration was abundantly clear when he wrote: "Service here is idiotically dull. I am near to my spiritual death." (21 August) "I am leading the thoroughly dull life of a hermit, and into the bargain I am in the stupidest thing God ever created – railway service!" (27 September) "I have somewhat more work with my company; we do so-called 'technical duty' from 8–11 a.m. and from 2–5 p.m. It is terribly futile." (27 October)[15] Then he finally received word concerning his application and was posted to *Flieger-Ersatz-Abteilung* 2 at Adlershof for pilot training on 12 November 1914. Wasting no time, he arrived there the next day. Adlershof itself was actually where advanced pilot training occurred and the military aviation school at Johannisthal, situated just opposite *FEA* 2, was where early instruction took place. Out of four possible Johannisthal groups that were centered around Jeanin, LVG, Albatros and Rumpler aircraft, Immelmann was assigned to the LVG unit. Due to his prior technical training and knowledge, however, he was also allowed to attend some of Adlershof's instructional courses (e.g., engine, aircraft construction, navigation, meteorology). By 20 November, he was up in the air on training flights: "I made several ascents today with my instructor. Four of them, altogether. Flying is a remarkable business. I think the finest moment is the one when you leave the ground. All the jolting stops then. Going into a glide is less pleasant; it is like being in a lift."[16] He had his first run at the controls himself on 21 November.[17] On 31 January 1915, Immelmann took off on his first solo flight. He successfully completed his first pilot's examination on 9 February and the second one just two days later on the 11th. A request went out from *Armee-Flug-Park* 3 at Rethel for replacement pilots on 4 March; so Immelmann left Adlershof on 9 March and arrived at Rethel three days later. There he completed his third and final pilot's exam, taking off on the required long distance flight on 27 March but not returning to Rethel until two days later due to inclement weather and a crash at *FFA* 24's Lille airfield that broke both of his plane's wheels and one undercarriage strut.[18] On 12 April 1915, Immelmann was given his first frontline assignment with *Feldflieger-Abteilung* 10 at Vrizy. After his plane had been modified for war duty (i.e., "metal sheets under the tank and under the two seats, and fixed racks to store the bombs, a map-board, an altimeter and a few other gadgets."), he took off the next day to familiarize himself with the area.[19] When he returned to base and touched down, one wheel and an undercarriage strut broke once again. He picked up a replacement aircraft on 16 April but then pranged it (touched the ground with his left wing, breaking an interplane strut) upon landing. Therefore, from Immelmann's own reports home, there is evidence to support Prof. Johannes Werner's assertion that Immelmann had gained the "reputation of being a specialist in the art of crashing his machine on landing" (see p.13 above). Willy Aschenborn went as far as to state that this is what caused Immelmann to be sent away (albeit temporarily) from frontline duty. One other incident may have contributed as well. During an artillery spotting mission, the artillery unit's CO watched as Immelmann's machine inexplicably sideslipped into a power spin and dropped 500 meters before recovery. He telephoned the next day to see if anyone was hurt, but probably spoke with *FFA* 10's CO as well. At any rate, Immelmann was indeed posted out of *FFA* 10 after just 13 days of service and sent back to Germany to join a new unit, *Feldflieger-Abteilung* 62, being formed at Döberitz.

As already noted in our Boelcke discussion (see p.13 above), *FFA* 62 eventually made its way to Douai, arriving there around 18 May 1915. Immelmann billeted with *Lt*. Erhardt von Teubern and *Lt*. Oswald Boelcke: "It soon transpired that we suit one another very well. None of us smoke, and we practically never touch alcohol, but we are very fond of cakes."[20] Immelmann alternated between Teubern and *Hptm*. Ritter as his observers; and it was with Teubern that he experienced his first air combat on 3 June 1915. During a reconnaissance mission, their unarmed LVG B.I was attacked by a Farman. Teubern insisted upon completing his photography run so their plane was holed several times before Immelmann was able to break away: "At last Teubern is finished. It is a horrible feeling to have to wait until one is perhaps hit, without being able to fire a shot oneself!"[21] As a reward for their patience in finishing the mission, Immelmann and Teubern were both given the Iron Cross, 2nd Class the same day by their CO, *Hptm*. Hermann Kastner.

Immelmann graduated from flying an LVG B.I to an LVG B.II on 13 June 1915 after it was handed down to him by Oswald Boelcke, who had moved on to an armed 150 hp LVG C.I. Unlike the other B.IIs, Immelmann's had a sting of its own because a captured French machine gun had been mounted in front of the forward cockpit (where the observer rode in this type). Immelmann had it slightly repositioned according to his preference and promptly went on several missions with a decidedly less defensive attitude. He was forced to land with a holed petrol tank after one, but succeeded in chasing two enemy planes away in another. His aggressive side was beginning to emerge.

After Anthony Fokker and *Lt*. Otto Parschau demonstrated Fokker's new E.I fighter plane at Douai on 23 June 1915, two of the type (3/15 and 13/15) as well as a practice machine (probably an A.I/M.8) were left in *FFA* 62's care. Boelcke took one of the E.Is up the next day and switched to flying it almost exclusively by 7 July. Around this time, Boelcke's C.I was again handed down to Immelmann in recognition of his fighting spirit: "When I told an acquaintance in Lille, who is also an airman, that I was flying a 150 h.p. fighter, he asked me with great amazement: 'Are you the senior pilot in your section?' That I am certainly not. Of the nine pilots in our section six are older than me, and only two younger (I mean in flying age)."[22] He almost lost the plane, however, less than a week later. On 12 July, Immelmann became disoriented by thick clouds and a snow storm, and when he had to make a forced landing near Trooz, his propeller and left wheel broke. Not one to give in easily, Immelmann had the plane dismantled and transported (first by manpower, then by a horse-drawn cart and finally by hooking it up to a mail train) back to Douai where it was so quickly repaired by a team of mechanics that he was able to report the next day to *Hptm*.

Above: Immelmann proudly displays the Iron Cross, 1st Class he was awarded right after his first victory.

Kastner – who believed the plane to be a total write-off – that the "machine is serviceable and in her tent."[23] Toward the middle of July, Immelmann was assigned the task of preventing enemy aircraft from spotting German artillery conducting a frontline bombardment. He did so successfully, chasing at least two aircraft away. As a result, he was awarded Saxony's Friedrich August Medal in Silver on 15 July. He then learned on 20 July that he had been promoted to *Leutnant* as of 14 July.[24]

Fighter Pilot
Immelmann Summary: "My first war flight in a Fokker *Eindecker* on 1 August, likewise first victory. At first sometimes flew a biplane, other times an *Eindecker*, but only an *Eindecker* from the end of September. Became an officer on 15 July 1915, promoted to *Oberleutnant* on 18 April 1916. Mentioned for the first time in the official military communiqués with four victories on 11 October, awarded the *Pour le Mérite* upon the eighth victory, got the Commander's Cross of the Military St. Henry Order upon the twelfth. Shot down 15 Englishmen by the beginning of June, of

Above: The wreckage of Immelmann's third victory, shot down on 21 September 1915.

which 14 fell on our side of the lines – a number that I alone can look back upon."

Intrigued by the E.I *Eindecker* fighter, Immelmann asked Oswald Boelcke on 30 July 1915 to take him up in the practice machine Fokker had left behind the previous month. After watching "how he handled the controls" and returning to earth, Immelmann conducted several solo flights, claiming that he made five perfect landings after each.[25] Then he took up one of the E.I fighters the next day and practiced firing the machine gun at a ground target. On 1 August, he was scheduled for an early morning reconnaissance flight in his LVG C.I; however, poor weather postponed it and he went back to bed. Then around 5:45 a.m., he was roused by the loud noise of antiaircraft fire and exploding bombs. Their airfield was under attack: "There were at least ten enemy machines in the air. In the distance we saw Boelcke in pursuit of another monoplane. Since I am not a lazy man, I got the other Fokker out of its shed and buzzed off... I was up to 2,400 by the time I was almost over Douai, and then I saw two other opponents and Boelcke... all three were heading for Arras... Suddenly I saw Boelcke go down in a steep dive. As I learnt later, he had a bad gun stoppage, so that he could not fire another shot. I was about halfway between Douai and Arras when I caught sight of a third machine a long way ahead of me... Then I saw him drop bombs on Vitry... I climbed a bit and made for him. I was about 80–100 metres above when 50 away I saw the huge French markings quite clearly – blue, white and red rings... The two others were now heading for me, and they were still high above me. So I had to act quickly. I dived on him like a hawk and fired my machine gun. For a moment I thought I was going to fly right in to him. I had a gun stoppage when I had fired about 60 shots; that was most unpleasant because I needed both hands to remove it, which meant that I had to go on flying without handling the controls. It was a new and strange experience for me, but I managed it. The same thing happened twice more in the course of the fight. Meanwhile the enemy was making for Arras. I flew alongside of him and cut off his line of retreat by forcing him into a left-hand turn, which put his machine in the direction of Douai. In the course of these manoeuvres we went down to about 400 metres. In the intervals of firing I heard faintly the rattle of machine guns of the other foemen who were above me. I tried to keep my machine vertically above my opponent's, because no biplane can shoot straight up. After firing 450–500 shots in the course of a fight which lasted about 8–10 minutes, I saw the enemy go down in a steep glide. I went after him. I could fire no more shots, because my machine gun failed me. When I saw him land, I went down beside him, climbed out and went up to him. There was no one in the neighborhood, and I was unarmed. Would the inmates offer resistance? It was an unpleasant moment. I called out when still some distance away: 'Prisoners!' Then I saw for the first time that there was only one man in the cockpit. He held up his right hand as a sign that he would offer no resistance. I went up to him. I shook hands and said: 'Bon jour, monsieur.' But he answered in English. 'Ah, you are an Englishman.' 'Yes.' 'You are my prisoner.' 'My arm is broken; you shot very well.' Then I saw for the first time that his left arm was badly wounded. I helped him out of the machine, laid him on the grass, took his gloves off and cut away the sleeves of his leather coat, tunic and shirt. A bullet had gone through his forearm. Cars were arriving from all directions, for they had been watching the fight in Douai. I sent someone off at once for a doctor... My shooting was good. Two shots in the propeller, but none in the engine; three in the petrol tank, four or five in the fuselage and six in the wings, while all the instruments such as altimeter, anenometer and rev-counter were shot to pieces. Further bullets had hit several bracing wires and control-cables, the bomb rack and the left wheel – almost everything was shot to pieces. There were about 40 hits on the machine."[26] Immelmann's first victim was Lt. William Reid of RFC No.2 Squadron in BE.2c 1662. After the war, Reid recounted how Immelmann's opening salvo had shattered his left arm in four places. He had then nosed down to try to head for his lines but his engine stopped before going much farther. He also mentioned that Immelmann had taken the trouble to fly over the lines the same afternoon to drop the English a note at St. Pol detailing his fate.

Through the rest of August and into September,

Above: Max Immelmann's photo is taken by Friedrich August III, King of Saxony, on 15 November 1915 during a visit to *FFA* 24's airfield near Lille.

Immelmann alternated between his LVG biplane and *Eindecker*, generally flying the former in the morning and the latter in the evening. Indeed, his second victory, which he may have shared with Boelcke on 10 September, occurred quite late in the day and he had to land in the dark afterwards. Immelmann broke the pattern on 21 September, however, and took off in his E.I around 9:00 a.m. to fly cover for an unarmed aircraft on artillery spotting duty. It was his 25th birthday and he gave himself his third conquest – an English BE.2 – as a present.

By the morning of 7 November 1915, Immelmann had added another two to his tally. Then while on patrol that afternoon: "Flying in the profoundest peace, I did several circles round Arras, and then I saw an enemy airman crossing the lines near Lens. He was about 1,000 metres below me; consequently I was able to push the machine down as I flew towards him and so approached at great speed. I came to within 100 metres of him. The Englishman had not yet noticed me, so I held my fire. I waited until within 60 metres and then gave him 50 rounds, whereupon he went down in a left-hand turn. An Englishman flying about 20 metres higher shot at me, but with no success. I went down after the machine I attacked. After he had dropped several hundreds of metres in a glide, he fell. Shortly afterwards I landed near him. The machine was completely wrecked, both inmates were dead. I pulled the two bodies out of the wreckage. One had six mortal wounds, the other two bullets in his head. All their bones were broken. The aviation staff officer, who had watched the fight, came also to the scene of the crash. I was congratulated on all sides. When everything of military value had been removed from the two bodies, they were taken away for burial. I took off and flew home."[27]

An eyewitness on the ground gave this account: "It was around 4:00 p.m. My orderly had just brought some good coffee into my quarters (which really weren't that bad), and I was just about to enter a record of my early mobilization days into my war diary when I heard the chatter of machine guns outside. I at first attached no particular significance to this... but when my orderly shouted I hurried outside into the garden and saw an airplane falling a short distance away with a second descending in a banking flight nearby. 'The Frenchman's done for!' shouted a woman next to me who had watched the whole thing. People immediately poured out of their accommodations from all sides. Military police, mounted officers, automobiles all made their way to the spot where the airplane had just come down. After a short time, two other planes landed in the vicinity. When I arrived, a large circle of soldiers from all branches of service had already flocked around the airplane. In the center of the circle lay the heavily wrecked enemy airplane, of English origin with small English flags and large French cockades. The two occupants, young English

Above: The King of Saxony (just right of center, showing left profile) and some of his staff converse with a member of *FFA* 24 (back to camera) during his visit to their airfield.

officers, lay dead beside it – the one with two fatal head shots, the other dead immediately after the crash due to the severe injuries it had caused. A physician provided for the quick removal of the two corpses in one of the available automobiles. *Leutnant* Immelmann stood among a group of officers beside the rubble of the plane, telling them details about the fight's course of events. The enemy combat plane, equipped with three machine guns, had been in pursuit of two German fliers and did not notice him until quite late when he dove upon it like a bird of prey and delivered the fatal shots at very close range. A short battle of life and death, two men against one; but Immelmann had aimed well. The opponent sought to descend in spirals, but then fell steeply. A short time later, Immelmann landed just a few meters away from the fallen enemy. He described all this to us in simple, short words but his high-pitched voice still contained some of the excitement of the dangerous battle. He did not have a lot of time, and probably little desire, to tell the story. After a brief goodbye, he went to his airplane – which had so faithfully borne him in the battle – got in, shouted a few funny words to the soldiers standing in the way of his takeoff, and then the airplane started moving amidst the cheers of those standing around. He crossed over us twice, waived, and a final cheer accompanied him on his trip toward Douai... The two other planes ascended too, the automobiles rattled away, the 'mounted ones' got on their horses and the service men gradually made their way back to their accommodations."[28]

On 15 November 1915, Immelmann was ordered to *Feldflieger-Abteilung* 24's airfield outside of Lille to put on a flying demonstration for his homeland's king, Friedrich August III of Saxony. Many press members attended as well and Immelmann was photographed at various times in front of the wreckage of his fourth victory, with the men of *FFA* 24 and in front of his E.II 37/15. Movie films were taken too that were later shown in German cinemas across the country. But the highlight for Immelmann was his audience with the King, who did two extraordinary things to honor his aviator subject. First: "He went straight up to me, inspected and expressed surprise at Englishman No.4, and then took a photo of myself standing in front of this machine – just imagine, the King snapped me himself." Then, following Immelmann's flying demonstration which he closed with a ground level pass, saluting the King as he went by: "When the machine came to a standstill, the King snapped me again. Then he came up to me and expressed his appreciation of what he had seen. Suddenly he grew plainly embarrassed and said: 'It's really fine what you have done, hm, hm, hm, hm. I've brought you something as well. Hm, hm, hm. There's a monoplane on it, tcha, a monoplane. It's a plate from Meissen. Yes, Meissen porcelain. Here, would you like to have it? Here, if you'd like to have it.' And

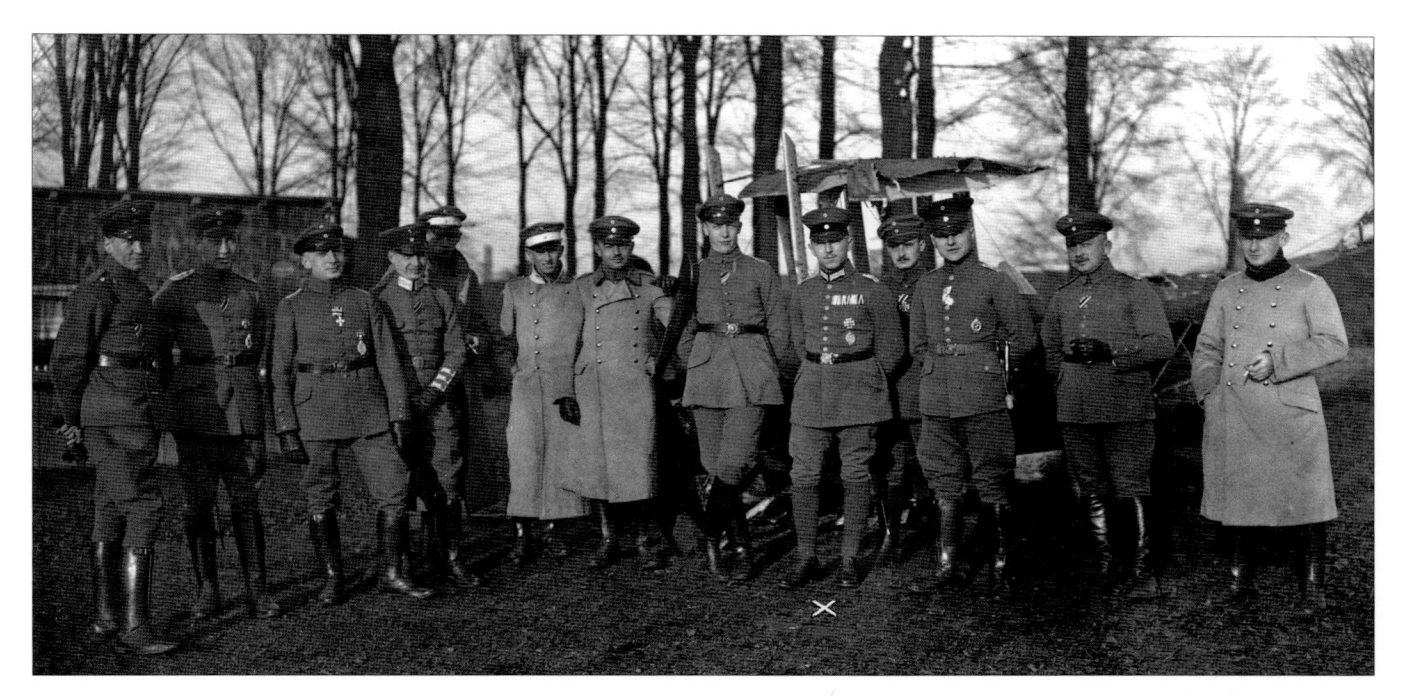

Above: Immelmann poses along with members of *FFA* 24 in front of the remains of his fourth victory during the same visit.

with that he handed me a plate of Meissen porcelain, on which there was a charming picture of a fight between a German '*Taube*' and an enemy biplane... His Excellency von Wilsdorf then told me that the plate was a special mark of distinction, because the King went into the Royal Porcelain Factory at Dresden himself and chose it. It is really very nice of him. Such a present is certainly a far more personal thing than an order."[29]

A special event to raise funds to buy Christmas presents for German airmen was scheduled for 28 November at Leipzig's Mockau airfield. Its promoters requested Immelmann's attendance and his superiors acquiesced. While there, he was spotted by newspaperman E. Goldfreund who wrote this account: "An icy-cold November day. Snow lies ankle deep on the Leipzig airfield; nevertheless one sees thousands of freezing people, wrapped in heavy furs, coming and going there with eyes shining in expectation of an event: Immelmann!... Immelmann was the sensation of the day. Army command had released him in order to help the charitable event be a special success. I can still see him there before me today, how he came along with his brother, who was almost a head taller, and Director Fokker. No 'hero' with a stern, forceful appearance, but a kind, young man as bright and cheery as one of only 25 years can look. And then after that introduction, when I had a chance to speak with him for a few minutes, he briefly and concisely explained how he attained his success: 'You go up, hit one if you're lucky, and the plane falls down.' He had hardly delivered these words – a testimony to his great courage – when he saw his mother coming to meet him and he rushed to her, beaming with happiness. At that moment he was just her son... To his own great disappointment, he was not allowed to fly because such participation was forbidden to all military aviators; but whether he flew or not, the public, now aware of him, demanded to see him. In an instant he was surrounded by thousands of people, one of the crowd gave three cheers for him, the rest joined in jubilantly; and then he was suddenly seized by four strong arms, raised up on shoulders and carried away over the field amid rejoicing that did not want to end... But he used a favorable moment to vanish and elude any further ovations – he fled to his mother. Nothing marked Immelmann's modest heroism better than that moment."[30]

Immelmann had once cautioned his mother: "You must not expect that there will be a decoration for every machine shot down."[31] Yet this is close to what was taking place. After his first victory (1 August) he received the Iron Cross, 1st Class (2 August); following the second (26 August), the Albert Order, Knight 2nd Class (10 September); after the fourth (10 October), the Military St. Henry Order (13 October); and following the sixth (7 November), the Royal Hohenzollern House Order (c.10 November). After returning to the Front a day early from his leave on 6 December 1915, Immelmann shot down his seventh plane on 15 December, and the Military Merit Order, 4th Class came to him just three days later. Even Immelmann, however, did not

Above: Immelmann and his mother at the 28 November 1915 fundraising event held at Leipzig's Mockau airfield.

Above: Immelmann poses on Leipzig's Mockau airfield, holding a silver cup that was presented to him by the city's mayor.

imagine what was in store for him and Boelcke after they had each brought down their eighth victories on 12 January. Immelmann's conquest was Vickers FB.5 5460 of RFC No.11 Squadron, manned by 2nd Lts. Herbert T. Kemp (pilot) and Sidney Hathaway (observer). *Gefreiter* Störck, an eyewitness from a nearby railway group, recounted: "At 9:15 a.m. on 12 January 1916, an enemy plane flew over our station. *Leutnant* Immelmann took off directly and was immediately in combat. The whole thing lasted three to four minutes when the enemy plane suddenly caught fire and had to land. I hurried right to him to see everything that was going on. It was a French plane with two English crewmen, one of whom lay dead beside the plane with stomach wounds. The blood soaked through his clothes. The other sat on a bundle of straw, smoking a cigarette, and had two glancing wounds to the head and neck. Then *Leutnant* Immelmann arrived and wanted to shake hands with the Englishman, who refused with the words: 'I cannot shake your hand because you shot my comrade.'"[32] Hathaway was the dead man and Kemp was taken to a field hospital. Later the same evening: "As is the custom when the section celebrates a joyful event, our leader spoke a few words, but this time his speech was livelier and gayer than usual. I cannot remember everything he said, because I was too excited with my pleasure. I did not really listen until at the end of his short speech. He said something about a milestone in the history of aviation and a turning point and recognition in high places, but finally the big word came out: 'His Majesty the Emperor has been graciously pleased to confer the highest war order, the *Pour le Mérite*, on the two victors in aerial warfare.' I was dumb. I should have thought it a joke if my section-leader had not said it in front of all our officers. I couldn't eat or drink anything that day; I didn't know whether I was awake or dreaming. I never slept as badly as that night. I dreamt only about the *Pour le Mérite*."[33] Boelcke recalled: "We were just sitting down to dinner when I was called to the telephone. There the chief's [i.e., *Feldflugchef* Hermann Thomsen] adjutant announced himself and congratulated me on receiving the *Pour le Mérite*. I thought he was having a joke with me, but he informed me that the order had been bestowed on Immelmann and myself by a telegram from His Majesty. Great were my surprise and joy. Then I went in to the dining room, but said nothing and just sent Captain Kastner to the telephone. He came back and made a public announcement about our decorations; at first everyone was very astonished, then there was great rejoicing."[34] The next day, the *Heeresbericht* reported to all of Germany and the world: "*Leutnante* Boelcke and Immelmann each shot down an English plane, one northeast of Tourcoing and the other near Bapaume. His Majesty the Kaiser has bestowed the *Orden Pour le Mérite* upon these intrepid officers in recognition of their extraordinary achievements."

Congratulatory telegrams and letters poured in from all over the country. Immelmann's and Boelcke's admirers ranged anywhere from the highest nobility to the humblest of country children.

Above: Two postcards that featured photographs taken at Pieperhoff's Leipzig studio that Immelmann gifted to his mother (he pointedly referred to them in a letter home as "me with and without cap"). The first was produced by E.P. & Co. around February 1916 whereas Neue Photographische Gesellschaft (NPG) offered the second posthumously in July 1916.

Above & Left: Two views of Immelmann's eighth victim, Vickers FB.5 5460. The first shows the body of its unfortunate observer, 2nd Lt. Sidney Hathaway, laying near the partially-burned aircraft.

Above: Immelmann (right foreground) on 30 March 1916 right after his receipt of the Commander's Cross of the Military St. Henry Order. Crown Prince Georg of Saxony, who bestowed the decoration on Immelmann, stands at center while *Gen*. Maximilian von Laffert (left foreground) looks on.

It seemed as though everyone wanted to contact or spend time with the nation's newest heroes, and the airmen dined with the likes of Ludwig III, King of Bavaria and his son, Crown Prince Rupprecht. But just as the celebrations began to subside, Boelcke and Immelmann's partnership was broken up when Boelcke (now with nine victories) was sent away to Montmédy on 21 January to participate in preparations for the Verdun offensive.

Immelmann seems to have reacted to his increasing fame somewhat differently than his comrade. At first, he had similarly eschewed any form of overt publicity, as when he wrote on 28 October 1915: "Fame also brings its burdens. I can't get it into my head that I have done anything particular. Above all, do not part with any of my letters or photographs. You will fall into my eternal disgrace if anything of mine is published. The public citation which His Majesty had approved and granted will suffice for me."[35] Nevertheless, he also offered in the same letter: "Now I shall no longer object to being written up in the papers, since I have seen how everyone at home follows my successes. It is amazing." While on leave in Germany in late November 1915, Immelmann had several photographs taken of himself at the Pieperhoff Studio in Leipzig as a Christmas gift for his mother. By February 1916, one of them was being presented for sale to the public on a postcard produced by E.P. & Co. of Leipzig. Since it had originally been privately commissioned, it seems likely that E.P. & Co. had at least received Immelmann's tacit approval, if not direct involvement, to do so.

Around the same time, multiple photos of

Above & Right: Immelmann's twelfth (FE.2b #6352) and thirteenth (BE.2c #4116) victories, respectively.

Immelmann taken at Douai (or nearby Lille) began to be marketed by Willi Sanke's postcard firm – the beginning of its famous airmen series. Several included facsimiles of Immelmann's signature that were even updated upon his promotion – another indication that he may have actively cooperated in the venture.[36] By April 1916, Immelmann was no longer averse to having his family sell some of his photographs, as when he instructed his mother: "I am sending you here 6 pictures of me. One is on fine paper with my own signature. It is intended for you. The others are less valuable because the signature is printed. You can do whatever you want with these other 5 pictures. Either give them to relatives or let them be sold for a high price (perhaps by Franz). 30 to 40 marks apiece."[37] And then in May 1916, Immelmann reversed his ban on publishing his letters when he gave Berlin's August Scherl company permission to reproduce many of his letters to his mother in a booklet entitled *Meine Kampfflüge*. His reasons were disclosed in the book's forward: "Letters wanting to persuade me to put my wartime experiences down in writing have been increasing daily from all sides. At first, this was not very appealing to me because in my opinion there is enough written in this war by professional and amateur pens; and what is on average provided to readers as 'air battles and aviator letters' is often irresponsible and to me seems better suited to confusing the layman, rather than clarifying for him, what aviation work is really all about. It was this fact that eventually induced me to try to offer as true an account of my aviation experiences as possible. So the letters below, in which I tell my mother of my activities, should be published. In order to save young readers from any disappointment, it should be stated in advance that they are the sober recordings of a passionate flier."[38] Thus Immelmann, unlike Boelcke, appears to have accepted and actively supported his own publicity; but this is not to say that he was excessive in this respect. Perhaps Ernst Sieverts, who served with Immelmann in *FFA 62*, summed it up best: "At first, he was not pretentious. Later, after receiving many orders, he became a bit vain... But he was an extraordinary man, his weaknesses were harmless and he was always the dear comrade."[39]

The weather in February 1916 was mostly abysmal and neither Immelmann nor Boelcke had many opportunities for further conquests. March, however, was a different story and both men finished it tied with tallies of 13. For Immelmann, it closed on an even more special note when he was awarded Saxony's Commander's Cross of the Military St. Henry Order (2nd Class) on 30 March. It was personally presented to him by Crown Prince Georg of Saxony and the distinctive honor was never again repeated during the war either for an airman or a *Leutnant*. Immelmann wrote his mother: "To me as a Saxon the Commander's Cross is a higher Order than the '*Pour le Mérite*.'"[40] Indeed, from then on he displayed it below his collar in place of his *Pour le Mérite*, which was now relegated to a lower position.

In early April, Georg Queri, correspondent for the "Berliner Tageblatt" newspaper, visited Immelmann at the Front: "Immelmann is a modest, reserved soldier with large, quiet eyes. The great flier emerged from the former Saxon cadet who came to the theater of war in January 1915, first reconnoitering in a biplane and then rising up as a crack shot in the *Eindecker* fighter. His very first *Eindecker* flight was a success. An Englishman circled over the German airfield. The small apparatus spiraled up in a hurry and the Englishman fell as his prize. Immelmann does not speak about the dangers of combat. Danger and luck are personal experiences that he keeps locked up within himself. As a flier he acts boldly and quickly and talks as sparsely as level-headed men do. His face lights up, however, and his voice grows warmer when he speaks of

Above: Immelmann, wearing signs of all his decorations except one (the Imtiaz Medal in Silver), converses with Crown Prince Rupprecht of Bavaria. Therefore this picture was likely taken within weeks, if not days, of Immelmann's death.

the Kaiser's handwritten letter. He got immense pleasure from the fact that the Emperor was in the process of congratulating him on his twelfth victory just as his *Kampfstaffel* reported his thirteenth to headquarters. The Emperor crossed out 'twelfth' and wrote 'thirteenth' above it, and it is said that the Kaiser remarked: 'One cannot write as quickly as Immelmann shoots.'

Immelmann's comrades are also pleased with his successes. They say he can positively smell when there is good game to hunt. Boelcke possesses this peculiar talent as well. Both men feel the desire to go hunting, ascend and suddenly find the enemy. Their extraordinarily fast airplanes can reach an opponent even when he is fleeing and then their shooting skills usually decide the matter. As a result, the English squadrons have become somewhat nervous. One of the last Englishmen faced by Immelmann was a quite courageous soldier who kept on firing even as his shot up plane was going down. He let go of the machine gun and clenched both his fists at his enemy as he fell into the depths below... Immelmann is known as an extremely hard-working flier. Consequently, the competent and brave officer has received quite a number of extraordinary honors. Among the ten medals that he has earned are the *Pour le Mérite* and Saxony's highest decoration. He naturally receives many letters from the homeland. The commander of his unit smilingly told me that he will need to provide a special orderly to open Immelmann's letters as well as a hardened soldier to read through the many homemade poems, and probably a handwriting expert to sign Immelmann's autograph."[41]

Right after his investiture with the Commander's Cross of the Military St. Henry Order, Immelmann mentioned to Crown Prince Georg of Saxony that he was contemplating abandoning his current reserve status in the military. Now that he was famous and serving as a role model, Immelmann felt he should remain a pilot officer after the war and do so as a member of the full-time, active army. With encouragement from the Crown Prince, Immelmann sent in his reenlistment papers and was not only reinstated in the active army but also promoted to *Oberleutnant* on 18 April 1916. As a further bonus, he regained all but a few days of the seniority he had lost when he had gone into the reserves. That evening, the event was celebrated in *FFA 62*'s mess where Immelmann was serenaded by a band and cheered by hundreds of soldiers outside. Then came victory 14 on 23 April. Just two days later, however, Immelmann was given a sober reminder of the grim side of his career: "I had a nasty fight in the air today. I took off at about 11 a.m. and met two English biplanes southward of Bapaume. I was about 700 metres higher and therefore came up with them very quickly and attacked one. He seemed to heel over after a few shots, but unfortunately I was mistaken. The two worked splendidly together in the course of the fight and put eleven shots into my machine. The petrol tank, the struts on the fuselage, the undercarriage and the propeller were hit. I could only save myself by a nose-dive of 1,000 metres. It was not a nice business."[42]

May started slowly for Immelmann who complained about the lack of opportunites despite good weather. This changed on 16 May when he downed a Bristol Scout that had gone after two of *FFA* 62's LVGs. Then a harbinger of his eventual fate occurred on 31 May: the interruptor gear on his E.IV's machine guns failed during an air engagement. According to brother Franz, the same thing had happened the previous March, but Max had been able to land under relatively good control then because both propeller blades had been evenly severed. This time was different though. Only one was sawn off and the resulting vibrations generated

Above: Immelmann entertains representatives from five neutral countries (Switzerland, Holland, Spain, Argentina and Denmark) at his Douai airfield on 31 May 1916. *Lt.* Albert Oesterreicher is at far left.

by the lopsided propeller almost tore the engine from its mounts and fouled the plane's rudder control. Franz wrote: "Then his Fokker suddenly reared up with a terrible jerk, which was followed by a horrible shaking and jolting... Weird tremors accompanied the final revolutions of the engine which went round very irregularly with the driving force of its 14 cylinders and only half a propeller, until at last a violent jerk brought it to a standstill, and at the same moment the machine whirled down into the depths over its left wing."[43] Immelmann barely made it down alive. Outwardly, he appeared none the worse for wear when a group of military men representing neutral Switzerland, Holland, Spain, Argentina and China visited *FFA* 62's airfield a few hours later. Inwardly, his narrow escape might have added to the stress of the past six months of active duty. *Lt.* Erwin Böhme, who at the time was serving with *Kampgeschwader* 2 near Landres, noted in a letter to his fianceé shortly after Immelmann's death: "Recently the poor chap was very much at the end of his rope – he really should have been forced to take more time off."[44]

FFA 62 was able to mount only two patrols in early June before the unit was broken up. On 12 June 1916, its Fokker contingent was separated and reformed as *Kampfeinsitzer-Kommando* 3 (also known as *KEK* Douai) after which the remaining two-seaters departed for the Eastern Front on 15 June. The weather cleared on 17 June and *KEK* 3 made its first two forays against the enemy without result. The next day would be very different.

Late on the afternoon of 18 June, Immelmann and three other Fokker pilots ascended to intercept a group of FE.2b's from RFC No.25 Squadron. During the ensuing dogfight, the pilot of FE.2b 6940, Lt. Clarence E. Rogers, and his observer, Sgt. H. Taylor, were both wounded. Rogers managed to bring the plane down safely near Bucquoy but died of his wounds soon after. Immelmann's E.IV was also damaged by enemy fire and put out of commission for the rest of the day. A few hours later, another No.25 Squadron group crossed the lines and five Fokkers took off to meet them. Immelmann was in a spare fighter, E.III 246/16, when he waded into the fight. He attacked FE.2b 4909 with pilot Lt. John R.B. Savage and observer Airman 2nd Class T.N.U. Robinson as its crew. Then a second FE, manned by 2Lt. C.R. McCubbin (pilot) and Cpl. J.H. Waller, came to their aid. McCubbin later reported: "Savage, whilst proceeding towards them suddenly signalled that he was returning. He was much nearer the Fokkers than I was, and they apparently noticed this as well, and one dived on him immediately. I was flying much higher than they were and immediately dived on the one that was by this time on Savage's tail, but did not open fire. The other two got on my tail, with the result that you had a string

Above: The wreckage of Immelmann's Fokker E.III 246/16 at its crash site. The tail section and wings broke away in midair and fluttered to the ground separately.
Left: The remains of Immelmann's Fokker E.III 246/16 collected and stored in an aircraft shed.

of machines all diving down. Savage's machine suddenly got out of control, as the Fokker had been firing at it, and Savage's machine went down. By this time I was very close to the Fokker and [the pilot] apparently realised we were on his tail, and he immediately started to do what I expect was the beginning of an 'Immelmann' turn. As he started the turn we opened fire and the Fokker immediately got out of control and went down to earth."[45] The wings and tail of Immelmann's Fokker broke away, after which the nose and forward fuselage, carrying its hapless passenger, plummeted to earth near Sallaumines. Savage and Robinson, both wounded, put down outside of Lens and Savage later died of his wounds.

Controversy ensued. McCubbin and Waller naturally believed that they had shot Immelmann down, and they were subsequently awarded the Distinguished Service Order and Distinguished Service Medal, respectively, for that deed. German authorities believed differently, however. An investigation concluded that Immelmann had again shot himself down because of a machine gun interruptor gear failure. They cited clear evidence

Above & Below: Two images of Savage and Robinson's FE.2b 4909, dubbed "*Baby Mine*" on its nose, after it put down near Lens. The image below shows what remained of the tail section of Immelmann's Fokker E.III being carried past the captured aircraft in a car.

Left: Immelmann's body lies in state in the garden of Army Hospital A.

of a sawn-off propeller blade at machine gun level – something that appears to be observable in many of the surviving photos of the E.III's wreckage. Oswald Boelcke, who went to Douai and must have spoken with the investigators, told his family: "Immelmann lost his life by a silly chance. All that is written in the papers about a fight in the air, etc. is rot. A bit of his propeller flew off; the jarring tore the bracing wires connecting up with the fuselage, and then that broke away."[46] Eyewitnesses on the ground stated that shortly after attacking a plane, Immelmann's *Eindecker* started to make strange tumbling movements, rearing up and then diving down, until the tail section broke off. Indeed, what McCubbin and Waller may have witnessed when they opened fire was Immelmann's already stricken plane performing much the same as his other had on 31 May when it too lost a propeller blade – rearing "up with a terrible jerk" and then whirling "down into the depths over its left wing." But Immelmann's former mechanic, Georg Junginger, also related this often-overlooked tidbit during a postwar interview: "The conclusion of the investigation of Immelmann's Fokker after the fatal crash was that bullet holes through the prop blade caused Immelmann's death. According to Mr. Junginger, bullets hitting the prop blades was a common occurrence for the Fokker E planes and, after 2 or 3 hits, the props were changed. Immelmann's prop had not been repaired."[47] So it is possible that Immelmann's already damaged blade had broken off during the fight. Whatever the actual cause, the inescapable result was that one of Germany's leading airmen was now dead.

Franz Immelmann stated that his brother shot down two planes on the day of his death, yet it turns out that neither was ever officially credited to him and his official total remained at 15. Several theories have been offered as to why. Some sources believe that since Immelmann was not alive to make his claims, they could not be processed. As we shall see, this may have been partly accurate. Max Mulzer's combat report for 18 June makes it clear that he believed he shot down 4909: "Around 10:00 on the evening of 18 June, I had an air combat with an English Vickers biplane northeast of Lens. The enemy airplane worked quite skillfully and tried to get me with continual machine gun fire. I constantly pursued the opponent and finally, after several turns, forced him to land, whereby I descended to about 150 meters... I had fired approximately 500–600 shots during the course of the battle."[48] McCubbin and Waller lost sight of 4909 after Immelmann's plane began to go "out of control," and it is quite possible that what they perceived as Savage and Robinson going down actually was Savage putting 4909 into a dive as a ruse to escape Immelmann's fire. Mulzer may have then caught up to 4909 and finished the job. In that case, Immelmann's only victory that day would have been FE.2b 6940 – a success that went unrecognized because he was no longer alive to complete the claim process.

The Immelmann Summary's final line stated: "Shot down 15 Englishmen by the beginning of June, of which 14 fell on our side of the lines – a number that I alone can look back upon." This at first seems curious, since Oswald Boelcke had amassed 18 victories by 21 May. Other statements by Immelmann, however, clear up the matter. On 28 October 1915, he wrote: "[Boelcke] claims to have

Right: The *Ordenskissen* used to display Immelmann's decorations during his funeral ceremonies. At the top is his *Pour le Mérite*. Below that on his medals bar, left to right: Military St. Henry's Order, Knight's Cross; Albert Order, Knight 2nd Class with Swords; Friedrich August Medal in Silver; Iron Cross, 2nd Class; Royal Hohenzollern House Order, Knight's Cross with Swords; Military Merit Order, 4th Class with Swords; Hamburg Hanseatic Cross; Friedrich Cross, 2nd Class. Then comes his Military St. Henry's Order, Commander's Cross, 2nd Class, flanked by the War Medal ("Gallipoli Star") at left and Iron Cross, 1st Class at right. Below them are his Pilot's Badge and Imtiaz Medal in Silver.

shot down five enemy machines, but one of them landed on its own territory. If I counted all those, I should have at least seven."[49] On 16 March 1916: "Then I heard in the evening that Boelcke had shot down a Frenchman on the 12th and another on the 13th. These two, however, did not fall on German territory, but on French ground."[50] Finally, on 7 May: "*Monsieur* Navarre's nine machines are a whopping lie. Five of them landed behind our lines. It is certainly proper in the end to count those which fall behind enemy lines because the main point is that the airplane and crew have been put out of action."[51] Immelmann was of the opinion that downed aircraft able to land behind their own lines should not be counted as victories since they could live to fight another day. He also evidently believed that of Boelcke's 18 successes, at least five or more had returned to their own territory. Hence the 14 he brought down behind German lines was "a number that I alone can look back upon."

Max Immelmann's coffin lay in state in the garden of Douai's War Hospital A "...in the centre of a grove of laurels and cypresses, where it was surrounded by wreaths and covered with a sea of roses. It was flanked by four pillars, crowned with iron braziers, from which glowing flames rose up to heaven."[52] A large host of people, comprised of royal dignitaries, high officers and common soldiers, gathered there on 22 June to bid farewell. Among their ranks was Oswald Boelcke, who had flown over from Sivry and spent the prior evening in the mess with Franz Immelmann talking about his brother. At 5:00 p.m., a brief ceremony was held at which the 6th Army's Aviation Staff Officer, *Maj.* Friedrich Stempel, delivered the eulogy. As he finished, Fokker

Right: *Lt*. Max Mulzer, carrying Immelmann's *Ordenskissen*, leads the procession out of the hospital garden as Immelmann's coffin is borne to a gun carriage waiting outside.

Left: Immelmann's coffin is carried to the rail car that later transported it to Dresden.

Above: Immelmann's mother Gertrud (center) and sister Elfriede (shaking hands with officer) greet his coffin after its arrival at Dresden-Neustadt train station. Another relative, possibly his aunt Elsa Boetzel, views the coffin inside the rail car.

Right: Immelmann's coffin and wreaths are loaded into a large, ornately carved hearse as his family stands nearby (center).

aircraft flew by overhead. Then *Lt.* Max Mulzer, Immelmann's fellow fighter pilot and friend, carried the deceased man's decorations on a black, striped pillow in front of the coffin as it was carried out of the garden to a carriage for transportation through the streets of Douai. The entire procession followed on foot and upon reaching Douai rail station, once again paid their respects to the fallen airman as his body was loaded into a rail car. Roses were dropped from aircraft above, a three volley salute was fired and a band played the 'Ballad of the Good Comrade' as the train pulled out to begin its journey to Dresden.

The following are descriptions of the Dresden

Above: The horse-drawn hearse carrying Immelmann's remains rolls down Dresden's streets as it makes its way to Tolkewitz's Johannes cemetery.

ceremonies: "Immelmann's remains arrived at the Dresden-Neustadt train station on 24 June 1916. It was closed off by a company of soldiers from *Grenadier-Regiment Kaiser Wilhelm II Nr.101*. Many thousands waited outside of the station's main building... sincere mourning could be read on all their faces. Not a word was spoken. Silence... the deceased's mother and sister appeared at the main building, where many officers had assembled. One had placed Immelmann's decorations on a cushion. After the family members had arrived, twelve men from *Jäger-Bataillon Nr.13* lifted the coffin, which was plain and unadorned, from the freight car... Many large wreaths, in which pieces of Immelmann's airplane had been interwoven, covered the coffin. It was lifted onto a hearse drawn by four horses and began to make its way along the street. The crowd swelled to even greater numbers. Thousands became ten thousands. Boy Scouts formed an honor guard on both sides of the street...It was just a little before 6 p.m. when the impressive procession arrived at Tolkewitz's Johannes cemetery."[53] Immelmann's final service took place at the cemetery's Memorial Hall the next day, 25 June: "The coffin stood on a marble base. It was invisible under a mountain of flowers... the ceremony began with the '*Niederländischen Dankgebet*'. This was followed by the organ prelude '*Jerusalem, du hochgebaute Stadt*' and then the speech of pastor Dr. Kautzsch of the Reformed Church (Immelmann was a catholic, but rejected the catholic clergy's known principle banning cremation funerals)... During the speech a Zeppelin approached the hall and circled the funeral place several times. It sank down quite low and dropped two bouquets of roses to earth that were collected and placed at Immelmann's coffin. After the clergyman finished, Mayor Blüher of Dresden began to speak and paid tribute to the city's son. At the special request of the family, the military band played '*Deutschland, Deutschland über alles*' and all the attendees joined in."[54] Immelmann's remains were then cremated and placed in the cemetery's Grove of Urns.

Endnotes

[1] A reproduction of the handwritten letter appears in Malkowsky, *Vom Heldenkampf der deutschen Flieger*, pp.18–21. A transcript of the letter was printed in Friedrich Frei, *Unser Fliegerheld Immelmann†*, pp.10–12.

[2] Claud Sykes' translation of Immelmann's biography refers to their "little sister" (p.16), implying that Elfriede was younger than the two boys. The original German's diminutive forms "*Schwesterlein*" and "*Schwesterchen*" ("little sister" or "baby sister") evidently were not used literally but rather as terms of endearment – a common German practice – because Max clearly stated that he had "*eine ältere Schwester*" ("an older sister") in his letter to Malkowsky.

[3] The White Stag sanatorium's emblem, designed by artist Ludwig Hohlwein, was used as personal aircraft insignia by *Pour le Mérite* recipients Rudolf Windisch (a fellow Saxon) and Carl Degelow.

[4] *Eagle of Lille*, p.20; *Adler von Lille*, p.15.

[5] Kranzler, *Bezwinger der Luft*, pp.8–9.

[6] *Eagle of Lille*, pp.20–21; *Adler von Lille*, p.15.

[7] Ernst Sieverts, a comrade of Immelmann's in FFA 62, disclosed: "He was raised as a vegetarian but in the field, he did eat meat although his real love was 'whole mountains of excellent cake' which he lit into each afternoon (he was a real trencherman; this was his only vice; apart from that, he was very frugal)." O'Connor, *Aviation Awards of Imperial Germany in World War I* 6, p.376.

[8] *Eagle of Lille*, p.22; *Adler von Lille*, p.16.

[9] *Adler von Lille*, p.16; *Eagle of Lille*, p.23 had a slightly different translation than the one given here.

[10] *Eagle of Lille*, p.28; *Adler von Lille*, p.24.

[11] *Eagle of Lille*, pp.30–31; Adler von Lille, p.26.

[12] *Eagle of Lille*, p.33; *Adler von Lille*, p.29.

[13] *Eagle of Lille*, p.45, incorrectly printed the date as 8 August where *Adler von Lille*, p.42, as well as Immelmann's 16 November 1914 letter, gave 10 August.

[14] There is plenty of confusion here. *Eagle of Lille*, p.46, incorrectly printed the date as 12 August where Immelmann's 16 November letter in *Adler von Lille*, p.43, gave 20 August. (Franz Immelmann had also stated earlier that the call-up occurred on 18 August and that his brother reported the next day.) Immelmann's letter, written closer to the actual event, has been chosen herein as the more accurate. Having said that, the Immelmann Summary says that he was called up into *Eisenbahn-Regiment* Nr.1 whereas Immelmann's 16 November letter says it was to his "old regiment," which would have been Nr.2. The two units are clearly distinguished in the Immelmann Summary.

[15] *Eagle of Lille*, pp.42, 44–45; *Adler von Lille*, pp.38–39, 42.

[16] *Eagle of Lille*, p.49; *Adler von Lille*, pp.45–46.

[17] In a letter dated 24 April 1916, he stated: "I did not make my first flight on the 8th but the 21st of November." (*Eagle of Lille*, p.191; *Adler von Lille*, p.166) Seeing that he had already gone up several times in aircraft by then, 21 November must have been the first time he had been allowed to take over the controls from his instructors – hence his "first flight" meaning actually flying the plane. This finds support in his 2 December 1914 letter where he says: "I have been

[18] The Immelmann Summary gives 26 March as the date he passed Pilot's Exam 3; but his own letter of 31 March states that he took off on 27 March and did not return to Rethel until 29 March. Therefore, 29 March is the date used herein.
[19] *Eagle of Lille*, p.72; *Adler von Lille*, p.65.
[20] *Eagle of Lille*, pp.98–99; *Adler von Lille*, p.88.
[21] *Eagle of Lille*, p.102; *Adler von Lille*, p.90.
[22] *Eagle of Lille*, p.108; *Adler von Lille*, p.95.
[23] *Eagle of Lille*, pp.108–12; *Adler von Lille*, pp.95–98.
[24] Though his later summary gives the date as 15 July, his letter of 31 July specifically states: "During my absence a telegram arrived: 'Ensign Immelmann promoted to lieutenant as from July 14th, 1915.'" (*Eagle of Lille*, p.115; *Adler von Lille*, p.101) This letter, written much closer to the actual event, has been chosen as being more accurate.
[25] Willy Aschenborn gave a different account: "Although Immelmann could just barely bring the machine down intact after his first two school flights, he was able to return from his third flight with the news of his first victory..." ("*Als Beobachter Boelckes im Westen*", p.218) Boelcke similarly reported that Immelmann had "considerable difficulty" in landing the plane (see p.13 above).
[26] *Eagle of Lille*, pp.117–19; *Adler von Lille*, pp.103–05.
[27] *Eagle of Lille*, p.152; *Adler von Lille*, p.132.
[28] *Bezwinger der Luft*, pp.24–26. Lt. Owen V. LeBas and Cpt. Theodore D. Adams were the unfortunate crew of BE.2c 1715 of RFC No.10 Squadron. Cpt. C. Gordon Bell had accompanied them in a Bristol Scout and been distracted by an Aviatik biplane while Immelmann shot them down. Perhaps this Aviatik and another were the "other two airplanes" mentioned in the eyewitness account.
[29] *Adler von Lille*, pp.133–34. The translation given here is the complete version, unlike that found in *Eagle of Lille*, pp.154–55.
[30] *Unser Fliegerheld Immelmann†*, pp.24–27.
[31] *Eagle of Lille*, p.144; *Adler von Lille*, p.125.
[32] *Unser Fliegerheld Immelmann†*, p.28. Immelmann left out Kemp's refusal to shake hands in his letter to his mother and instead related that Kemp, after Immelmann had been introduced to him, responded with: "You are well known to us. Your victory today is another fine sporting success for you." (*Eagle of Lille*, p.168; *Adler von Lille*, p.146.)
[33] *Eagle of Lille*, p.169; *Adler von Lille*, p.147. For some reason, the original final two sentences in *Adler von Lille* were omitted from *Eagle of Lille's* translation, so they have been reinserted here.

[34] *Knight of Germany*, pp.142–43; *Boelcke: der Mensch*, p.131.
[35] *Eagle of Lille*, p.144; *Adler von Lille*, p.126. Presumably, the citation Immelmann referred to here was the report of his fourth victory that appeared in the *Heeresbericht*.
[36] For more details on these photographs and postcards, see Bronnenkant, *The Imperial German Eagles* 1 and 3.
[37] This 16 April letter is in this writer's collection. The original German and its translation appear in Bronnenkant, *The Imperial German Eagles* 2, p.202.
[38] Immelmann, *Meine Kampfflüge*, pp.5–6.
[39] O'Connor, *Aviation Awards of Imperial Germany* 6, p.376. Sieverts also noted: "He loved to have himself photographed each time he got a new medal... After the award of the *Pour le Mérite*, he was called 'Your Exalted Excellency.'"
[40] *Eagle of Lille*, p.189; *Adler von Lille*, p.164.
[41] *Vom Heldenkampf der deutschen Flieger*, pp.22–23. Immelmann's first assignment as an airman during the war came in March 1915, not January.
[42] *Eagle of Lille*, p.194; *Adler von Lille*, p.168. Immelmann might have tangled with BE.2c's from RFC No.15 Squadron who were reconnoitering the German trench system being constructed along Ablainzeville-Irles-Le Sars-Flers. One of them, manned by Lt. AB Adams (pilot) and 2Lt. CR Robbins, reported being attacked by and fending off Fokkers.
[43] *Eagle of Lille*, pp.201–02; *Adler von Lille*, p.174.
[44] Werner, *Briefe eines deutschen Kampffliegers*, p.30.
[45] Franks, *Sharks Among Minnows*, pp.100–01.
[46] *Knight of Germany*, p.178; *Boelcke: der Mensch*, p.163.
[47] *Cross & Cockade* 3:3, p.207. Boelcke did not specifically state that Immelmann had shot off his propeller, but only that a piece of it "flew off"[see original German] Does this support Junginger's assertion or was Boelcke merely protecting his parents from the notion of mechanical failure in the aircraft he flew?
[48] See Reinhard Kastner, "Leutnant Max Ritter von Mulzer" in *Das Propellerblatt* 17:2, pp.617–19.
[49] *Eagle of Lille*, p.143; this passage was omitted from the 1942 edition of *Adler von Lille*.
[50] *Eagle of Lille*, p.180; *Adler von Lille*, p.157.
[51] *Adler von Lille*, p.169. *Eagle of Lille*, p.196, has a slightly different translation than the one presented here. Immelmann was referring to French ace Jean Navarre, who was credited with nine victories as of 24 April 1916.
[52] *Eagle of Lille*, p.219; *Adler von Lille*, p.185.
[53] Heuer, *Held-Immelmann*, pp.92–93.
[54] *Vom Heldenkampf der deutschen Flieger*, pp.36–37.

Immelmann – The Aircraft
LVG B.I (318/15 & various unknown serial numbers) (21 November 1914 – 12 June 1915)

When Max Immelmann began his flight training at *FEA* 2 outside of Berlin on 13 November 1914, he found that the adjacent military aviation school at Johannisthal offered several options: "The pupils here are allotted to the various factories making L.V.G.'s, Albatroses, Rumplers and Jeanins... I have been allotted to the L.V.G. school, and am very pleased. The L.V.G. build beautiful biplanes which at present give the best results for lift, speed and climbing capacity."[1] LVG had developed the B.I before the war and adapted it for both training and reconnaissance duties after the conflict had begun. This is likely the type that Immelmann trained in and it seems that he stayed with the B.I for much of his pre-fighter pilot career. Indeed, Immelmann's biography included a picture of him, Im1, that was labeled: *"Als Flugschüler im L.V.G.-Doppeldecker in Johannisthal 1914/15."* ("As a flying student in an LVG biplane in Johannisthal, 1914–15.")

When he was assigned to *Armee-Flug-Park* 3 at Rethel on 12 March, Immelmann noted: "We have here L.V.G's, Albatroses and Gotha-*Taubes*. I fly an L.V.G."[2] He makes several LVG references up to the time he ferried one over to his new assignment, *FFA* 10 at Vrizy on 12 April.[3] After crashing that one, he was sent back to Rethel to pick up "a new machine," which sounded like a B.I too given Immelmann's description of it.[4] His stay with *FFA* 10 was brief and upon arriving at his new posting at Döberitz on 28 April, Immelmann learned he "...was to join a new section which was being raised to fly L.V.G. biplanes, and that this section would be No.62..."[5] Willy Aschenborn tells us that the new *FFA* 62 was only equipped with LVG B.Is before he and Boelcke managed to commandeer a B.II literally at the eleventh hour before their departure to the Front on 13 May (see p.13 above). Immelmann continued to fly a B.I alternating between *Lt*. Ehrhardt von Teubern and *Hptm*. Ritter as his observers. On 3 June, he and Teubern had their first air battle with an armed French biplane. Im2 is a snapshot of Immelmann and Teubern after that encounter and Im3 illustrates some of the damage done to their machine, LVG B.I 318/15, that day.[6]

LVG B.II 712/15 (13 June through 6 July 1915)

Immelmann apparently had to wait until Oswald Boelcke received *FFA* 62's first armed fighting machine, LVG C.I 162/15, on 13 June before he could upgrade to the LVG B.II. In this instance, it was B.II 712/15 – a hand-me-down from Boelcke, who had recently armed it with a captured French machine

Im1: Max Immelmann sits alone in the pilot's aft cockpit of a running LVG B.I during his flight training days at Johannisthal.

Im2–3: In the first image (above), *Fähnrich* Max Immelmann (left) and his observer, *Lt.* Ehrhardt von Teubern, pose in front of their LVG B.I 318/15 after having been attacked by an armed, French Farman biplane. The second image (right) shows some of the damage the plane sustained during the attack, which Immelmann described as: "When we landed, they counted our bullet-holes. There are about five or six harmless ones in the wings. A solitary one grazed our main spar, without breaking it. One shot went clean throught the engine's bed. The metal cowling which encloses the lower part of the engine looks like a sieve." (*Eagle of Lille*, p.102; *Adler von Lille*, p.90)

gun. Immelmann relocated the machine gun according to his own preferences and took pictures of his arrangement, as seen in Im4–5. Immelmann was thrilled and wrote on 25 June: "So now I have the little L.V.G., which can climb and fly much faster but is also somewhat more difficult to handle. I took this bus up to 3,200 on the very first day, and climbed to 3,500 several days afterwards. The next thing I did was to have the machine gun remounted where I thought best. We made such a good job of it that... the captain ordered a photograph to be taken and sent to the aviation staff officer as an example of

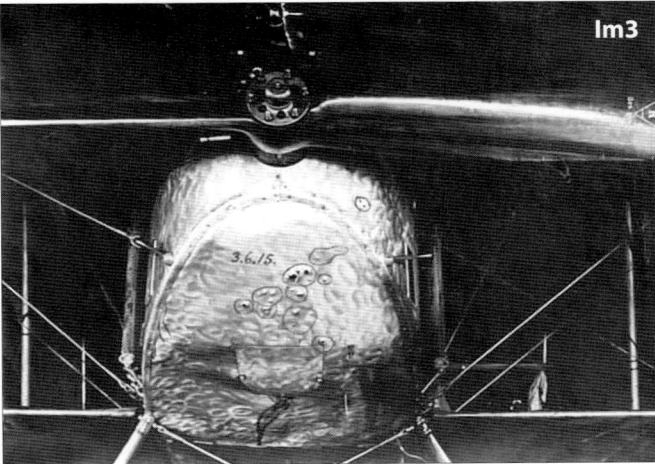

Im4–5: These photos of B.II 712/15 show how Immelmann refitted its machine gun. Two mounts were secured on either side of the observer's cockpit allowing him to reposition it as needed.

a particularly good mounting of a captured machine gun... I am sending you the snaps in this letter. The roller is a drum, on which is wound a steel belt with a hundred cartridges."[7]

Immelmann reported several fights in the machine but soon switched over to a more advanced model, again passed down to him by Boelcke.

LVG C.I 162/15
(7 July into August 1915)
On 17 July, Immelmann wrote: "I have got the 150 h.p. biplane fighter which became vacant when Lieutenant Boelcke took the one-seater fighter... With this fighter, which is one of the so-called C Machines, one can cross the lines and see an enemy machine approach without suffering from that feeling of definite inferiority which undoubtedly attacks anyone in one of the other machines without a machine gun... Things are going to be different now."[8] As we saw earlier, Boelcke informed us that this transfer took place as of 7 July (see p.15 above). Im6–7 are photos of Immelmann in what is believed to have been C.I 162/15, which he almost lost less than a week later while conducting a test flight following some repairs.

After Immelmann was introduced to the Fokker E.I monoplane in late June, he reported on 11 August: "Sometimes I fly the Fokker and sometimes the L.V.G.; I generally use the biplane in the morning and the Fokker in the evening. But it sometimes happens that I fly the biplane for three hours, land, get into the Fokker and fly it for an hour. Then the Fokker in the evening again, with airfights as the order of the day."[9] This tapered off as he and Boelcke became increasingly proficient in their *Eindecker* fighters. According to Immelmann's autobiographical letter to Emil Malkowsky (see p.67 above), he only flew *Eindeckers* in combat from the end of September 1915. On 18 May 1916, he unequivocally stated: "I never fly an L.V.G. on duty, but only to instruct a comrade."[10]

Fokker *Übungsmaschine* (practice machine)
(30 July 1915)

Fokker E.I 13/15
(31 July – 7 October 1915)
We already saw how *Fähnrich* Max Immelmann, intrigued with Fokker's new *Eindecker*, asked Oswald Boelcke on 30 July to take him up in a two-place practice machine (probably an A.I/M.8) that Fokker had left behind at *FFA* 62's Douai airfield earlier that month (see p.68 above). Immelmann, used to the aileron controls on LVG biplanes, needed to familiarize himself with the Fokker's wing-warping system. He related: "After watching him, I asked him to step out, and then I made five solo landings – all of them quite perfect... The next day I had a trial flight in one of the two war machines; I whizzed about in the air for 20 minutes and fired off 30 shots at a ground target, but unfortunately only hit it twice. Altogether, I felt very happy in that little bird."[11] Then came Immelmann's first victory on 1 August. Immelmann later related that this and his subsequent four victories were achieved with E.I 13/15: "My old 80 h.p. Fokker (the machine with the factory number E 13), in which I finished off my first five Englishmen, is going to be exhibited in the Zeughaus Museum in Berlin."[12] Im8 is a picture of Immelmann in E.13/15, whose serial number shows up under magnification. Compare it to B8 (see p.36). All aspects match – particularly the stain pattern on the fuselage though it appears slightly more advanced in Im8.

Im6

Im6–7: Max Immelmann poses in and out of the cockpit of an LVG C.I that was probably 162/15 – the plane in which Oswald Boelcke achieved his first victory and was later passed on to Immelmann.

Immelmann brought down his second on 26 August, followed by his third on 21 September: "And now I see plainly that he is falling. A thick cloud rises from the spot where he crashes, and then bright flames break out of the machine. Soldiers hasten to the scene... So I... decide to land, and come down close to the burning machine. I find soldiers attending to one of the inmates... I fly off again, to the accompaniment of rousing cheers from about 500 soldiers."[13] With this description in mind, we might have identified Im10 as a snapshot of Immelmann getting ready to leave that crash site if not for more photographic evidence and another passage's testimony. Im11–14 are images taken at various times of 13/15 on display at its final home in the Royal Saxon Army Museum in Dresden. Note the bullet hole that appears in the front of its cowling in both Im11 and Im12. It is the same hole that is circled in Im10. Immelmann describes a fight that he had two days after his third victory:

Im7

Im8. Max Immelmann in Fokker E.I 13/15. Its appearance is quite similar to that in B8, where Oswald Boelcke had used it to give rides to several visitors in early August 1915. **Im8blowup** inset.

"My Fokker was so badly shot about in a fight that it was unusable for a long time... In the course of the fray the fellow shot up my undercarriage, the bracing wires on the undercarriage, the oil tank, petrol tank, engine cowling, engine and fuselage."[14] This therefore begs the question: if his cowling had been so badly shot up, how could it have looked practically the same before and after his 23 September fight? Immelmann also tells us, after complaining that the result of his 23 September encounter was that both his and Boelcke's Fokkers were out of commission: "All of us here believe the French knew through their spies that both Fokkers were smashed up, for they have never been so impudent as they are now. They flew quite low – 16 machines at once. And I had to look on."[15] This negates any notion that he could have been flying a spare Fokker on the 23rd. Accordingly, Im10 must have been taken sometime after 13/15 had been repaired, though its cowling still bore the marks of the damage it had suffered on 23 September. We know Immelmann may have landed alongside his fourth victim on 10 October because he reported that "Prince Ernst Heinrich of Saxony arrived while I was still inspecting the machine," and a picture of him standing next to the plane's wreckage still in his flight gear is known to exist.[16] Im10 could have occurred at that time.

Fokker E.II 37/15
(8 October – at least 13 December 1915)
Immelmann's fourth fell on 10 October, followed by his fifth on 26 October. Though Immelmann claimed that they too were brought down with 13/15, we now know this was inaccurate. As described earlier (see p.38), Oswald Boelcke's E.II 37/15 was put out of commission shortly before he left *FFA* 62 in September and, according to Immelmann, it was not serviceable again until 8 October. It was then given over to Immelmann. This may or may not have been in time for him to have used it on the 10th, but we know that he did on the 26th. Im15–18 were taken after Immelmann had landed to inspect his victim and they clearly demonstrate that E.II 37/15 was his mount that day.[17]

Immelmann probably used E.II 37/15 to down his sixth victim on 7 November as well. He then took 37/15 with him when he went to Lille on 14 November to attend a court banquet given by Crown Prince Rupprecht of Bavaria. The next day, he gave a flying demonstration at *FFA* 24's field outside of Lille in front of Friedrich August III, King of Saxony, who had come to inspect the *Abteilung* and the remains of Immelmann's fourth victory (which had been moved to the unit's airfield). Multiple photographs were taken at the event with two ending up on widely circulated postcards. Im19 is one of them and displays Immelmann in front of E.II 37/15.

On 13 December, one week after returning from a home leave, Immelmann took up a "100 hp" Fokker for a test spin: "I had just taken off and climbed to 40–50 metres when the engine dropped considerably and finally went dead. I made a forced landing on a ploughed field. When I was almost touching the ground, the wheels went into a deep furrow, and the wind got underneath the steering surfaces (I had to land downwind) and lifted the tail up. Slowly but surely the machine turned over...I heard several

Im9: Immelmann poses in front of Fokker E.I 13/15. The serial number is barely visible on the original.

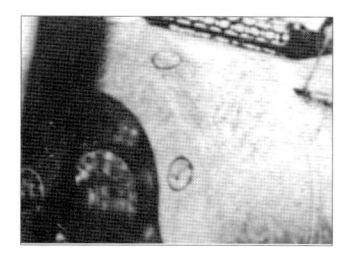

Im10blowup above.

Im10: Immelmann's E.I 13/15 sometime after most of the damage it had sustained in a 23 September fight had been repaired. Two bullet holes in the cowling, marked with circles, remained, however. The same type of circling of bullet holes is also evident in Im3 above. Note too that the German national insignia that covers some of the now heavily-stained fuselage seems relatively new. It was probably applied while 13/15 was in for repairs.

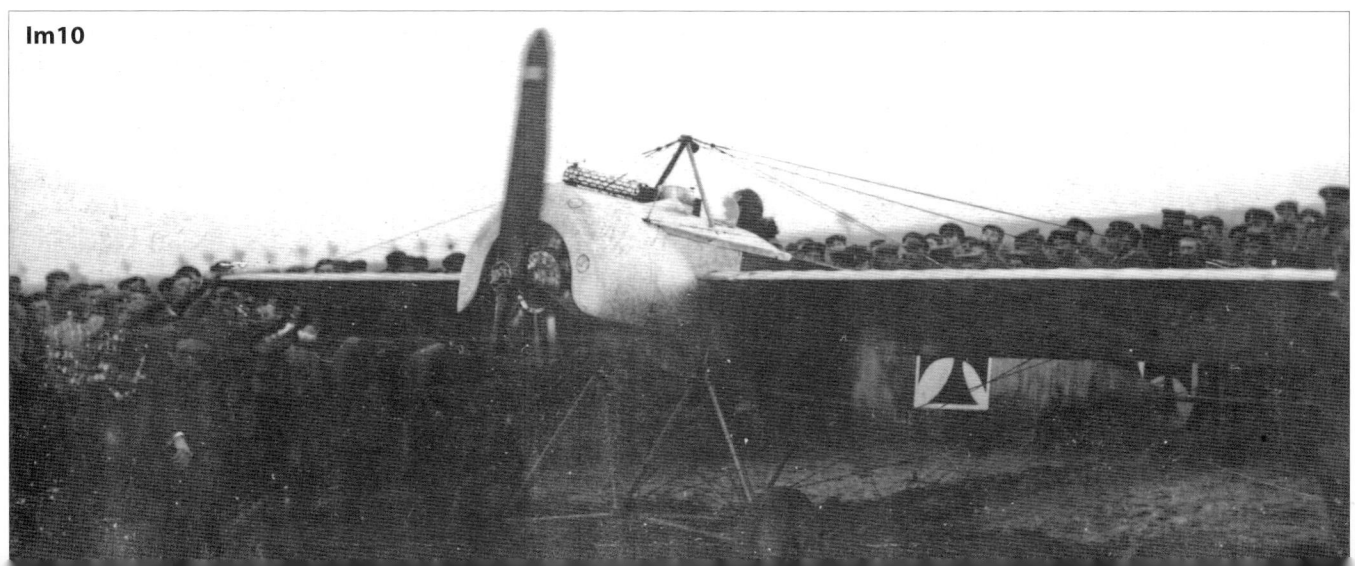

Im12blowup above.  **Im11blowup** above.

Im11–12: Immelmann's E.I 13/15 on display at Dresden's Royal Saxon Army Museum. The blowups show one of the same bullet holes in the cowling seen above.

mighty crashes, and then the bird was on her back...The propeller was broken, the engine shaft bent, the fuselage split down the middle and both steering surfaces broken. So it was almost a total write-off."[18] We cannot be sure if this was 37/15, because Immelmann then related that after being extricated from the wreckage, he took off in another "100 hp Fokker." At any rate, he used this other 100 hp fighter to down his seventh on 15 December 1915 and his eighth on 12 January 1916. Between those victories, on 5 January, Immelmann had tried his hand in Boelcke's E.IV 123/15 when he jumped into it to chase after a bombing squadron; but he ran out of fuel and had to land shortly afterwards.[19]

Fokker E.IV 127/15
(16 January – at least mid-March 1916)

Immelmann informed his mother: "I arranged for my 160 h.p. Fokker to be sent straight here. So my trip to Schwerin is off...The machine arrived on January 16th..."[20] Georg Junginger, during a postwar interview, spoke of his role in collecting Immelmann's first E.IV: "In the *Feld-Luftpark* 6b (Bavarian), I made the bird ready for service and,

Im13–14: Immelmann's E.I 13/15 on display at Dresden's Royal Saxon Army Museum.

Im15–18: Four photos taken at a field near Ecoust-Saint-Mein where Immelmann and his fifth victim set down after their encounter. The first shows VFB.5 5464 by itself. The next two capture Immelmann and E.II 37/15 nearby it. The final shot has Immelmann working on the plane (in flight gear near the nose) in front of an interested crowd of soldiers. He was unable to take off, however, because the fuel he needed to replenish his almost exhausted supply did not arrive until after dark. He therefore returned to Douai via automobile, towing 37/15 behind him.

Im18

from there, *Lt*. Immelmann flew the plane to the airfield at the Front. I informed Immelmann of my experience with the 160 PS engine and he told me that I was now his personal mechanic."[21] Numerous photographs and Fokker's records tell us that it was E.IV 127/15.[22]

By the time of his 5 February letter, Immelmann

had been unable to try 127/15 in action. On the 19th he reported that its engine had sustained "damages which took three days to repair. It would almost

Im19 Blowup (right): Serial number 37/15.

Im19: This photo, taken at *FFA* 24's airfield outside of Lille on 15 November 1915, was widely circulated on Sanke postcard number 347. Though heavily censored before publication (e.g., the engine and machine gun details were eradicated), the plane's serial number remained visible (see blowup above right). Note that the national insignia on the fuselage appears somewhat more weathered than it did in Im16.

Leutnant Immelmann an seinem Fokker-Flugzeug.

Im19

Im20: Max Immelmann sits in the cockpit of Fokker E.IV 127/15 on Douai airfield. A small, peaked structure that one photo album dubbed "*Das Immelmann-Haus*" pokes out from behind a hangar's wood door at right.

seem as if the English knew it, for on the morning of the 20th four of their machines flew over Douai on their way to Valenciennes. I had to look on inactively."[23] He was back in the air on 2 March, and despite his still "bad engine" managed to bring down his seventh.[24] Crown Prince Boris of Bulgaria visited *FFA* 62 a few days later (see Im21). This was followed by Immelmann's double victory on the 10th, which brought his total to 11. Immelmann left no doubt about which plane he had used: "I have now gained three victories in my new machine."[25]

Max's brother, Franz Immelmann, stated that: "Once in March, 1916, my brother sawed both his propeller blades cleanly off by shots from his own machine gun and was forced to make a hurried landing."[26] Im22 and Im23 show the results; and the unique gill-like feature on the plane (see Im21) tells us that the nearly fatal accident occurred in 127/15.

From here, we do not know how long it took for 127/15 to be repaired. In fact, we cannot be sure what type of *Eindecker* Immelmann flew for victories 12 through 14 because no specific clues appear in his biography. We do know, however, that he was flying a borrowed E.IV at the time of his 15th and last official victory on 16 May: "In the evening I wanted to test the climbing capacity of a new machine which a comrade had obtained a few days previously... after a while I saw three biplanes far below me... I discover that the upper one is a Bristol biplane and the lower two L.V.G.s... I dive still lower... I get him in my sights and take careful aim. I fire both machine guns simultaneously – 15–20 rounds from each."[27]

Fokker E.III 246/16 (18 June 1916)

On 18 June, the last day of his life, Immelmann and three other Fokkers engaged several FE.2s from RFC No.25 Squadron, bringing one down. After his return to base, another formation of seven planes from the same unit was reported as heading toward the front lines. "But the 160 h.p. Fokker is not serviceable; in the course of the afternoon's fight several of its struts have been badly shot about and the wings have been ripped; the repairs are not yet finished."[28] Immelmann therefore took off on his fatal flight in a spare E.III that many sources have cited as 246/16. The origin of this identification originally stemmed from the *Werknummer* ("factory number") visible in pictures of the plane's wreckage: 545. It is known that factory numbers 543 and 549 were assigned serial numbers 244/16 and 248/16, respectively, so it was assumed that 544 was 245/16, 545 was 246/16, and so forth.[29] Still, several examples exist where factory and serial numbers did not necessarily conform to a set sequence. Fortunately, aero historian Reinhard Zankl found a document that recorded that Fokker E.III 246/16 (100 hp Gnome engine #1159) belonging to *KEK* 3 of *FFA* 5b was

Im21: Boris, Crown Prince of Bulgaria (left) and Immelmann pose in front of E.IV 127/15 during a visit to *FFA* 62 in early March 1916. Two things are particularly noteworthy about this snapshot. First, 127/15 sports an apparently unique gill-like modification on its metal siding (just left of the Crown Prince's head). Second, the aft portion of the turtle deck is missing.

destroyed in a crash on 18 June 1916. Thus there is no doubt that this was the Fokker Immelmann died in.

To close this section, we will examine a well-known portrait of Immelmann posing in the cockpit of an 80 hp Fokker E.I. Im25 has appeared in many publications, several of which have identified the E.I as 13/15. Im26 is a lesser-known snapshot of the same plane. Both display its conspicuous markings: two diagonal stripes (possibly black and white) along the side of the fuselage just aft of the cockpit. Upon examination of the photographic evidence for E.I 13/15, however, it is difficult to reconcile when it would have borne such markings. Im8 and B8 show 13/15 during its early phase with a plain fuselage. Im10 depicts it at a later date when it bore the German national insignia on its fuselage; and Im11–14 demonstrate that it still carried that insignia, though repainted, in the same location when it was sent to Dresden's Royal Saxon Army Museum. These photos span 13/15's lifetime at the Front, yet none of them show any evidence of a set of diagonal stripes having once been applied to the fuselage (i.e., no overpainted patches are seen and the fuselage fabric's staining indicates it had not been replaced) – nor does it appear in Im25–26 that any national insignia had been overpainted.[30] It is also curious that the man at right in Im25 (wearing an *FFA* 62 armpatch) is carrying a sidearm, despite a multitude of German servicemen near the plane. This suggests two things: either it had landed near the enemy or it had been assigned special protection for some other reason. The former could mean that the E.I here was a spare that had temporarily been used by Immelmann and set down near the Front. The latter offers another more intriguing possibility. Several photos show that the E.I demonstrated by *Lt*. Otto Parschau at *FFA* 62's Douai airfield in June 1915 was marked with the same, though not identical, diagonal stripes. Was Im25–26's E.I one of the five monoplanes delivered to *FFA* 62 during Parschau's June–July 1915 stay there?[31] This might explain the special protection afforded by the armed guard because they were the first of their kind and still somewhat of a military secret at the time. If so, could Im25–26 even be snapshots of Boelcke's E.I 3/15? Fokker and Parschau left only two E.Is behind at *FFA* 62: 3/15 and 13/15. Boelcke posed in Immelmann's E.I 13/15 – why not the reverse? Such a conclusion has its appeal but must be relegated at this time to pure speculation.

Im22–23: Two snapshots of the nose of the E.IV in which Immelmann shot off both his own propeller blades sometime in March 1916. The presence of the gill-like feature in the first identifies the machine as 127/15 (first photo courtesy of Oliver Wulff).

Im24: One of a multitude of photos taken of the wreckage of Immelmann's E.III 246/16. In this case, the forward section that carried Immelmann to his death and the relatively intact tail section (that had separated in the air and fluttered down to earth some distance away) are photographed together after they had been gathered for temporary storage in a hangar. At left, one can see the neatly cut-off appearance of one of the propeller blades at machine gun level – one of the factors that led an investigation to conclude that he had once again suffered a synchronization failure.

Im25–26: Two photographs of Max Immelmann posing in an E.I marked with diagonal fuselage stripes. Though often identified by many sources as 13/15, this is by no means certain. (Im25 courtesy of Greg VanWyngarden).

Endnotes

[1] *Eagle of Lille*, p.47; *Adler von Lille*, p.44.
[2] *Eagle of Lille*, p.59; *Adler von Lille*, pp.54–55.
[3] E.g., "Then suddenly another machine broke through the clouds on our right. It was also an L.V.G…" (*Eagle of Lille*, p.63; *Adler von Lille*, p.57) and "Unfortunately, they had no L.V.G. parts; we had to go round to Section 5b to get the necessary spares." (*Eagle of Lille*, p.68; *Adler von Lille*, p.61).
[4] "…my observer and I obeyed them the next day and came back at 6 p.m. with the new machine, which can at least climb to 2,400 or 2,600, even if it is a bit slow." (*Eagle of Lille*, p.73; *Adler von Lille*, p.65.
[5] *Eagle of Lille*, p.83; *Adler von Lille*, p.74.
[6] Serial number from Grosz, *The LVG B.I*, p.22.
[7] *Eagle of Lille*, p.104; *Adler von Lille*, p.92.
[8] *Eagle of Lille*, p.107; *Adler von Lille*, p.94.

[9] *Eagle of Lille*, p.127; *Adler von Lille*, p.110.
[10] *Eagle of Lille*, p.199; *Adler von Lille*, p.172. We know of another time Immelmann piloted a biplane. Sometime in September 1915, his CO, *Hptm.* Hermann Kastner, asked Immelmann to fly him to Ghent. The engine gave out ten minutes into their flight and they had to make an emergency landing on a small field that ended in a wood. Immelmann intentionally 'pranged' his plane upon setting it down, hoping to shatter the landing gear and stop their forward momentum before hitting the trees. The ploy worked in part, breaking the right wheel, and then the plane "turned turtle" and ended up on its back with a broken propeller. (see *Eagle of Lille*, pp.136–37; *Adler von Lille*, pp.118–20) This writer has seen photos of the overturned plane in a private collection, and it appears to have been an LVG C.I. If it were 162/15, then it had received a new paint job because the entire plane was a much lighter color. By this time, *FFA* 62 had several C.Is in its inventory, so it is also quite possible that it was not 162/15.
[11] *Eagle of Lille*, p.116; *Adler von Lille*, p.102. Oswald Boelcke and Willy Aschenborn both independently reported, however, that Immelmann had "considerable difficulty" in landing the plane (see Immelmann – The Man, endnote 25).
[12] *Eagle of Lille*, p.181; *Adler von Lille*, p.157.
[13] *Eagle of Lille*, pp.134–35; *Adler von Lille*, p.117. His victim was BE.2c 2004, manned by 2nd Lt. S.W. Caws (pilot) and Lt. W.H. Sugden-Wilson of RFC No.10 Squadron. Caws never emerged from the burning wreck but Sugden-Wilson was thrown clear and survived.
[14] *Eagle of Lille*, p.138; *Adler von Lille*, p.120.
[15] Ibid. Boelcke's Fokker E.II 37/15 had suffered a devastating engine failure just before he was told of his transfer to *Brieftauben-Abteilung Metz (B.A.M.)* on 19 September. He left it behind for repairs so as Immelmann said, it too was not available to him after 13/15 had been put out of commission.
[16] *Eagle of Lille*, p.141; *Adler von Lille*, p.123. This writer has seen the photo, which is now in a private collection.
[17] This was RFC No.11 Squadron's VFB.5 5464, manned by Capt. C.C. Darley (pilot) and 2nd Lt. R.J. Slade. Darley tried – despite having been shot throught the right arm and thumb – to set the downed plane on fire, but was taken prisoner along with Slade before he could do so.
[18] *Eagle of Lille*, pp.160–61; *Adler von Lille*, pp.138–39.
[19] Immelmann wrote: "I did not know how much petrol there was in it, and it was all gone by the time I climbed to 2,500 metres." (*Eagle of Lille*, p.166; *Adler von Lille*, p.144) Boelcke, who had returned to *FFA* 62 around 12 December, said: "*Leider hatte Immelmann, der über Mittag auf dem Platz geblieben war, meine neue 160 PS Maschine - mit deren Hähnen er sich dann nicht zurecht gefunden hat – genommen, so dass ich mit einem alten 80 PS Reserve-Fokker fliegen musste.*" (*Boelcke: der Mensch*, p.129) ("Unfortunately Immelmann, who had stayed at the aerodrome over lunchtime, had taken my new 160 hp machine – whose [fuel] petcocks he was not yet correctly familiar with –so that I had to fly an old 80 hp reserve Fokker." (*Knight of Germany*, p.140, offers a slightly different translation than given here by this writer.) The implication is that Immelmann did not know how to switch over to the E.IV's reserve fuel tank. Incidentally, it is possible that *Lt.* Ernst Hess, who was credited with his first victory during this fight, had taken off in Immelmann's 100 hp Fokker – either that or Immelmann's 100 hp Fokker was for some reason unavailable that day.
[20] *Eagle of Lille*, p.170; *Adler von Lille*, pp.147–48.
[21] *Cross & Cockade* 3:3, p.204. Evidently, Boelcke's complaints about the unfamiliarity of *FFA* 62's mechanics with the new type (see p.41 above) were shared by Immelmann.
[22] Peter Grosz (*Fokker E.IV*, p.12), who examined Fokker records, said that 127/15 was only the third E.IV to leave Fokker's factory (after 122/15 and Boelcke's 123/15). It was accepted on 12 January 1916 and shipped out on 15 January.
[23] *Eagle of Lille*, pp.173–74; *Adler von Lille*, pp.150–152.
[24] *Eagle of Lille*, p.176; *Adler von Lille*, p.153.
[25] *Eagle of Lille*, p.181; *Adler von Lille*, p.157.
[26] *Eagle of Lille*, p.91; *Adler von Lille*, p.153. He did so again on 31 May, but that time sawed off only one blade.
[27] *Eagle of Lille*, pp.196-97; *Adler von Lille*, pp.170–71.
[28] *Eagle of Lille*, p.209; *Adler von Lille*, p.179.
[29] This writer is indebted to Josef Scott, *Eindecker* specialist, for this information.
[30] We can also see that two identification plates occur adjacent to one another near the cowling of Im25–26's E.I where only one appears in Im14; however, it is possible that one plate had been removed by the time the plane went on display in the museum.
[31] See p.35 above.

Above: Immelmann's E.III 246/16 at its crash site showing the crushed cockpit compartment (at right) from which Immelmann's body was extricated.

Above: Immelmann stands next to victory number seven, brought down on 15 December 1915. Its wreckage had been removed from its crash site on the wall of a house at Raismes and re-deposited at a German military site near Valenciennes.

Right: A grainy snapshot of Immelmann in the cockpit of his Fokker E.IV.

Below: Members of *FFA* 62 in front of "*Das Immelmann-Haus*" at Douai airfield. Left to right: unknown, von Schilling, two unknowns, Immelmann, unknown, *Hptm*. Hermann Kastner (CO), *Lt*. Ernst Hess, *Oblt*. von Gusnar, unknown, *Lt*. Albert Oesterreicher, *Oblt*. Maximilian von Cossel.

Immelmann – Military Service

Significant Dates

21 Sep 1890	born in Dresden
Mar 1911	admitted into army as *Fahnenjunker*
Apr 1912	certified as *Offizier/Degenfähnrich*; resigns from army; enters Reserves
20 Aug 1914	recalled into army service
12 Nov 1914	began flight training at Adlershof/Johannisthal
31 Jan 1915	first solo flight
9 Feb 1915	passed Pilot's Exam 1
11 Feb 1915	passed Pilot's Exam 2
9 Mar 1915	assigned to *Armee-Flug-Park* 3
29 Mar 1915	passed Pilot's Exam 3
12 Apr 1915	assigned to *Feldflieger-Abteilung* 10
26 Apr 1915	assigned to *Feldflieger-Abteilung* 62
14 Jul 1915	promoted to *Leutnant*
1 Aug 1915	first victory
12 Jan 1916	awarded *Pour le Mérite*
30 Mar 1916	awarded Commander's Cross of the Military St. Henry Order
18 Apr 1916	promoted to *Oberleutnant*
12 Jun 1916	assigned to *Kampfeinsitzer-Kommando* 3/Douai
18 Jun 1916	killed in action
22 Jun 1916	memorial service in Douai
25 Jun 1916	buried in Dresden

Service Units

4 Mar 1911–mid-Apr 1912	*Eisenbahn-Regiment* Nr.2
20 Aug 1914–11 Nov 1914	*Eisenbahn-Regiment* Nr.1
12 Nov 1914–8 Mar 1915	*Flieger-Ersatz-Abteilung* 2
9 Mar 1915–11 Apr 1915	*Armee-Flug-Park* 3
12 Apr 1915–25 Apr 1915	*Feldflieger-Abteilung* 10
26 Apr 1915–11 Jun 1916	*Feldflieger-Abteilung* 62
12 Jun 1916–18 Jun 1916	*Kampfeinsitzer-Kommando* 3/Douai

Right: Max Immelmann poses for a relaxed photograph.

The Immelmann

The "Immelmann Turn" has been linked to various tactical maneuvers including the *renversement*, *virage*, and half-loop followed by a half roll. According to *Pour le Mérite* airman Otto Bernert in an article he wrote in 1917, it was the English who used that term for what the Germans called a "*Pégoud-ischer Purzelflug*" or just "*Purzelflug*" (literally "somersault flight"), which was associated with pre-war stunt flier Adolphe Pégoud. Interestingly, neither Max Immelmann's correspondence nor his brother's biography of him ever mentioned an "Immelmann Turn," so it does not appear that Max himself believed he invented the maneuver.

Awards

27 Mar 1915	Pilot's Badge – Germany (date when passed final Pilot's Exam)
3 Jun 1915	Iron Cross, 2nd Class – Prussia
15 Jul 1915	Friedrich August Medal in Silver – Saxony
2 Aug 1915	Iron Cross, 1st Class – Prussia
10 Sep 1915	Albert Order, Knight 2nd Class with Swords – Saxony
13 Oct 1915	Military St. Henry Order, Knight's Cross – Saxony
c.10 Nov 1915	Royal Hohenzollern House Order, Knight's Cross with Swords – Prussia
18 Dec 1915	Military Merit Order, 4th Class with Swords – Bavaria
25 Dec 1915	*Ehrenbecher* – Germany
12 Jan 1916	*Pour le Mérite* – Prussia
15 Mar 1916	Hanseatic Cross – Hamburg
30 Mar 1916	Military St. Henry Order, Commander's Cross, 2nd Class – Saxony
8–18 May 1916	War Medal – Ottoman Empire
8–18 May 1916	Imtiaz Medal in Silver – Ottoman Empire
May/Jun 1916	Friedrich Cross, 2nd Class – Anhalt

Immelmann – Victory List

No.	Date	Aircraft	Location, Unit & Crew*
1	1 Aug 1915	BE.2c 1662	near Douai – RFC 2: 2Lt. William Reid (POW)
2	10 Sep	Nieuport 10	near Souchez – N15: *Cpt*. René Turin (WIA)
3	21 Sep	BE.2c 2004	near Willerval – RFC 10: 2Lt. Stanley W. Caws (KIA), Lt. William H. Sugden-Wilson (WIA/POW)
4	10 Oct	BE.2c 2033	near Verlinghem – RFC 16: 2Lt. John Gay (DOW), Lt. David Leeson (WIA/POW)
5	26 Oct	Vickers FB.5 5462	near Ecoust-Saint-Mein – RFC 11: Cpt. Charles C. Darley (WIA/POW), 2Lt. R.J. Slade (POW)
6	7 Nov	BE.2c 1715	near Quiéry-la-Motte – RFC 10: Lt. Owen V. LeBas, Cpt. Theodore D. Adams (b-KIA)
7	15 Dec	Morane Parasol 5087	Raismes– RFC 3: 2Lt. A.V. Hobbs, 2Lt. C.E.G. Tudor-Jones (b-KIA)
8	12 Jan 1916	Vickers FB.5 5460	near Tourcoing– RFC 11: 2Lt. Herbert T. Kemp (WIA/POW), Lt. Sidney Hathaway (KIA)
9	2 Mar	Morane BB 5137	near Somain – RFC 3: Lt. Charles W. Palmer (POW/DOW), Lt. Herbert F. Birdwood (KIA)
10	13 Mar	Bristol C Scout 4678	near Serre – RFC 4: Maj. Victor A. Barrington-Kennett (KIA)
11	13 Mar	BE.2c 4197	near Pelves – RFC 8: Lt. Gilbert D.J. Grune, 2Lt. Brian E. Glover (b-KIA)
12	29 Mar	FE.2b 6352	near Quéant – RFC 23: 2Lt. F.G. Pinder (WIA/POW), 2Lt. E.A. Halford (POW)
13	30 Mar	BE.2c 4116	near Serre? – RFC 15: 2Lt. Geoffrey J.L. Welsford (KIA), Lt. Wayland J. Joyce (WIA/POW)
14	23 Apr	Vickers FB.5 5079	Monchy-le-Preux – RFC 11: 2Lt. William C Mortimer-Phelan, 2Lt. William A. Scott-Brown (b-POW)
15	16 May	Bristol C Scout 5301	near Izel-lès-Equerchin – RFC 11: 2Lt. Morden M. Mowat (POW/DOW

*pilot listed first
b-   both occupants
DOW   died of wounds
ftl   forced to land
KIA   killed in action
POW   prisoner of war
WIA   wounded in action)

Below: Another view of Immelmann's Fokker E.IV 127/15, this time with a small dog on the inner port wing.

Pour le Mérite Winners by Date of Award

Recipient	Date of Award
Hptm. Oswald Boelcke	January 12, 1916
Oblt. Max Immelmann	January 12, 1916
Oblt. Hans-Joachim Buddecke	April 14, 1916
Lt. Kurt Wintgens	July 1, 1916
Lt. Max *Ritter* von Mulzer	July 8, 1916
Lt. Otto Parschau	July 10, 1916
Lt. Walter Höhndorf	July 20, 1916
Oblt. Ernst *Freiherr* von Althaus	July 21, 1916
Lt. Wilhelm Frankl	August 12, 1916
Hptm. Rudolf Berthold	October 12, 1916
Lt. Gustav Leffers	November 5, 1916
Lt. Albert Dossenbach	November 11, 1916
Oblt. Hans Berr	December 4, 1916
Rittm. Manfred *Freiherr* von Richthofen	January 12, 1917
Genlt. Ernst von Hoeppner	April 8, 1917
Oberst Hermann von der Lieth-Thomsen	April 8, 1917
Lt. Werner Voss	April 8, 1917
Oblt. Fritz Otto Bernert	April 23, 1917
Lt. Karl-Emil Schaefer	April 26, 1917
Oblt. Kurt Wolff	May 4, 1917
Lt. Heinrich Gontermann	May 14, 1917
Lt. Lothar *Freiherr* von Richthofen	May 14, 1917
Lt. Carl Allmenröder	June 14, 1917
Hptm. Ernst Brandenburg	June 14, 1917
Hptm. Paul *Freiherr* von Pechmann	July 31, 1917
Hptm. Adolf *Ritter* von Tutschek	August 3, 1917
Oblt. Eduard *Ritter* von Dostler	August 6, 1917
Fkpt. Peter Strasser	August 30, 1917
Lt. Max *Ritter* von Müller	September 3, 1917
Hptm. Rudolf Kleine	October 4, 1917
Lt. Walter von Bülow-Bothkamp	October 8, 1917
Lt. Curt Wüsthoff	November 22, 1917
Lt. Erwin Böhme	November 24, 1917
Lt. Julius Buckler	December 4, 1917
Lt. Hans Klein	December 4, 1917
Hptm. Eduard *Ritter* von Schleich	December 4, 1917
Hptm. Alfred Keller	December 4, 1917
Kptlt. Friedrich Christiansen	December 11, 1917
Lt. Heinrich Bongartz	December 23, 1917
Oblt. Hermann Fricke	December 23, 1917
Oblt. Hans-Jürgen Horn	December 23, 1917
Hptm. Bruno Loerzer	February 12, 1918
Lt. Heinrich Kroll	March 29, 1918
Kptlt. Horst *Freiherr* Treusch von Buttlar-Brandenfels	April 9, 1918
Oblt. Ernst Udet	April 9, 1918
Lt. Carl Menckhoff	April 23, 1918
Hptm. Hermann Köhl	May 21, 1918
Oblt. Erich Löwenhardt	May 31, 1918
Lt. Fritz Pütter	May 31, 1918
Oblt. Hermann Göring	June 2, 1918
Lt. Friedrich Nielebock	June 2, 1918
Lt. Rudolf Windisch	June 6, 1918
Lt. Wilhelm Paul Schreiber	June 8, 1918
Lt. Hans Kirschstein	June 24, 1918
Oblt. Otto Kissenberth	June 30, 1918
Lt. Emil Thuy	June 30, 1918
Lt. Peter Rieper	July 7, 1918
Lt. Fritz Rumey	July 10, 1918
Lt. Josef Jacobs	July 18, 1918
Lt. zur See Gotthard Sachsenberg	August 5, 1918
Hptm. Franz Walz	August 9, 1918
Lt. Josef Veltjens	August 16, 1918
Lt. Karl Bolle	August 28, 1918
Lt. Theo Osterkamp	September 2, 1918
Oblt. Fritz *Ritter* von Röth	September 8, 1918
Lt. Otto Könnecke	September 26, 1918
Lt. Walter Blume	September 30, 1918
Lt. Wilhelm Griebsch	September 30, 1918
Hptm. Leo Leonhardy	October 2, 1918
Oblt. Robert *Ritter* von Greim	October 8, 1918
Oblt. Jürgen von Grone	October 13, 1918
Oblt. Erich Homburg	October 13, 1918
Oblt. Albert Müller-Kahle	October 13, 1918
Oblt. Oskar *Freiherr* von Boenigk	October 25, 1918
Lt. Franz Büchner	October 25, 1918
Lt. Arthur Laumann	October 25, 1918
Lt. Oliver *Freiherr* von Beaulieu-Marconnay	October 26, 1918
Lt. Karl Thom	November 1, 1918
Lt. Paul Bäumer	November 2, 1918
Lt. Ulrich Neckel	November 8, 1918
Lt. Carl Degelow	November 9, 1918

Pour le Mérite Winners Alphabetically

Recipient	Date of Award
Lt. Carl Allmenröder	June 14, 1917
Oblt. Ernst *Freiherr* von Althaus	July 21, 1916
Lt. Paul Bäumer	November 2, 1918
Lt. Oliver *Freiherr* von Beaulieu-Marconnay	October 26, 1918
Oblt. Fritz Otto Bernert	April 23, 1917
Oblt. Hans Berr	December 4, 1916
Hptm. Rudolf Berthold	October 12, 1916
Lt. Walter Blume	September 30, 1918
Lt. Erwin Böhme	November 24, 1917
Hptm. Oswald Boelcke	January 12, 1916
Oblt. Oskar *Freiherr* von Boenigk	October 25, 1918
Lt. Karl Bolle	August 28, 1918
Lt. Heinrich Bongartz	December 23, 1917
Hptm. Ernst Brandenburg	June 14, 1917
Lt. Julius Buckler	December 4, 1917
Oblt. Hans-Joachim Buddecke	April 14, 1916
Lt. Franz Büchner	October 25, 1918
Lt. Walter von Bülow-Bothkamp	October 8, 1917
Kptlt. Horst *Freiherr* Treusch von Buttlar-Brandenfels	April 9, 1918
Kptlt. Friedrich Christiansen	December 11, 1917
Lt. Carl Degelow	November 9, 1918
Lt. Albert Dossenbach	November 11, 1916
Oblt. Eduard *Ritter* von Dostler	August 6, 1917
Lt. Wilhelm Frankl	August 12, 1916
Oblt. Hermann Fricke	December 23, 1917
Oblt. Hermann Göring	June 2, 1918
Lt. Heinrich Gontermann	May 14, 1917
Oblt. Robert *Ritter* von Greim	October 8, 1918
Lt. Wilhelm Griebsch	September 30, 1918
Oblt. Jürgen von Grone	October 13, 1918
Lt. Walter Höhndorf	July 20, 1916
Genlt. Ernst von Hoeppner	April 8, 1917
Oblt. Erich Homburg	October 13, 1918
Oblt. Hans-Jürgen Horn	December 23, 1917
Oblt. Max Immelmann	January 12, 1916
Lt. Josef Jacobs	July 18, 1918
Hptm. Alfred Keller	December 4, 1917
Lt. Hans Kirschstein	June 24, 1918
Oblt. Otto Kissenberth	June 30, 1918
Lt. Hans Klein	December 4, 1917
Hptm. Rudolf Kleine	October 4, 1917
Hptm. Hermann Köhl	May 21, 1918
Lt. Otto Könnecke	September 26, 1918
Lt. Heinrich Kroll	March 29, 1918
Lt. Arthur Laumann	October 25, 1918
Lt. Gustav Leffers	November 5, 1916
Hptm. Leo Leonhardy	October 2, 1918
Oberst Hermann von der Lieth-Thomsen	April 8, 1917
Hptm. Bruno Loerzer	February 12, 1918
Oblt. Erich Löwenhardt	May 31, 1918
Lt. Carl Menckhoff	April 23, 1918
Lt. Max *Ritter* von Müller	September 3, 1917
Oblt. Albert Müller-Kahle	October 13, 1918
Lt. Max *Ritter* von Mulzer	July 8, 1916
Lt. Ulrich Neckel	November 8, 1918
Lt. Friedrich Nielebock	June 2, 1918
Lt. Theo Osterkamp	September 2, 1918
Lt. Otto Parschau	July 10, 1916
Hptm. Paul *Freiherr* von Pechmann	July 31, 1917
Lt. Fritz Pütter	May 31, 1918
Lt. Lothar *Freiherr* von Richthofen	May 14, 1917
Rittm. Manfred *Freiherr* von Richthofen	January 12, 1917
Lt. Peter Rieper	July 7, 1918
Oblt. Fritz *Ritter* von Röth	September 8, 1918
Lt. Fritz Rumey	July 10, 1918
Lt. zur See Gotthard Sachsenberg	August 5, 1918
Lt. Karl-Emil Schaefer	April 26, 1917
Hptm. Eduard *Ritter* von Schleich	December 4, 1917
Lt. Wilhelm Paul Schreiber	June 8, 1918
Fkpt. Peter Strasser	August 30, 1917
Lt. Karl Thom	November 1, 1918
Lt. Emil Thuy	June 30, 1918
Hptm. Adolf *Ritter* von Tutschek	August 3, 1917
Oblt. Ernst Udet	April 9, 1918
Lt. Josef Veltjens	August 16, 1918
Lt. Werner Voss	April 8, 1917
Hptm. Franz Walz	August 9, 1918
Lt. Rudolf Windisch	June 6, 1918
Lt. Kurt Wintgens	July 1, 1916
Oblt. Kurt Wolff	May 4, 1917
Lt. Curt Wüsthoff	November 22, 1917

Index

Ackermann, Richard: 23
Adams, A.B.: 85
Adams, Theodore D.: 85, 103
Altengottern, Wolf Marschall von: 28
Althaus, Ernst von: 21, 44–45, 47–48
Antonioloi, Jean: 61
Aribert, Prince (Anhalt): 57
Arnim, Hans-Joachim von: 24, 31
Arnim, Sixt von: 28
Aschenborn, Willy: 8, 12–14, 23, 34–35, 66, 85–86, 100
Ball, Albert: 31
Baltzer, *Lt.*: 10, 23
Barker, Capt.: 15, 61
Barrington–Kennett, Victor A.: 103
Barton, F.: 61
Beckers, ?: 11
Bell, C. Gordon: 85
Below, Fritz von: 25, 28
Bieler, *Hptm.*: 14
Birdwood, Herbert F.: 103
Blanka, Nurse: 36–37
Bloem, Walter: 25–26
Blüher, Mayor: 84
Böhme, Erwin: 23–26, 29, 54, 58, 77
Boelcke, Karl: 28–29
Bölcke, Martin: 23, 28–29
Bölcke, Mathilde: 7, 9, 27–29
Bölcke, Max: 7–9, 27–29
Bölcke, Max Jr.: 7, 28–29
Boelcke, Oswald: 7–61, 65–68, 72, 74–76, 80–81, 85–86, 88–90, 92, 100, 112
Bölcke, Wilhelm: 10–12, 23, 28–29, 32–34, 48
Boetzel, Elsa: 63, 82
Bordas, Rodolphe: 61
Boris, Crown Prince (Bulgaria): 96
Bowen, E.G.A.: 61
Bowring, J.V.: 61
Bowyer, F.H.: 61
Brandis, Cordt von: 23
Brion, Henri: 61
Byrne, P.A.L.: 61
Cadet, Robert: 61
Cagninacci, Hubert: 61
Carre, E.M.: 61
Caws, S.W.: 100, 103
Cellière, Jean: 61
Chapman, Victor: 21
Collen, J.: 61
Cossel, Maximilian von: 101
Croneiss, Carl: 49
Darley, Charles C.: 100, 103

Degelow, Carl: 84
de la Rochefoucauld, Georges: 14, 30, 61
Dietsch, *Lt.*: 48
Dullin, Albert: 61
Eberling, Dr.: 29
Ernst Heinrich, Prince (Saxony): 90
Erskine, R.: 61
Essen, von: 40
Falkenhayn, Erich von: 23
Fiedler, Richard: 65
Finger, Pastor: 29
Fischer, Ludwig: 25
Förster, *Hptm.*: 22
Fokker, Anthony: 13, 24, 35, 39, 44, 58, 67–68, 97
Formilli, Geoffrey C.: 61
Frankl, Wilhelm: 25, 31
Fraser, W.: 61
Friedrich II, Duke (Anhalt): 29
Friedrich August III, King (Saxony): 69–71, 90
Gale, J.H.: 61
Galiment, Pierre: 61
Gay, John: 103
Georg, Crown Prince (Saxony): 74–75
Gleichen–Russwurm, *Hptm.* von: 25–26
Glover, Brian E.: 103
Gray, D.B.: 61
Gray, K.W.: 61
Grimmer, *Generalauditeur*: 62–63
Grune, Gilbert D.J.: 103
Gunther, Wolfgang: 24
Gusnar, *Oblt.* von: 101
Gutermuth, Hans: 48
Halford, E.A.: 103
Hartmann, *Lt.* von: 21, 31
Harvey, R.P.: 61
Hathaway, Sidney: 72–73, 103
Haxton, E.: 61
Hearson, J.G.: 15, 61
Helder, L.B.: 61
Herring, J.H.: 61
Hersing, Otto: 18
Hess, Ernst: 16, 40, 48, 101, 112
Hobbs, A.V.: 103
Hoeppner, Ernst von: 29
Hohlwein, Ludwig: 84
Holstein, Arnim von: 40
Imelmann, Hans: 25, 54–55
Immelmann, Elfriede: 62–63, 82, 84
Immelmann, Franz: 62
Immelmann, Franz Jr.: 62–63, 65, 75–76, 80–81, 96
Immelmann, Gertrud: 62–63, 72, 75, 82

Immelmann, Max: 13, 15–18, 22, 25, 30, 35, 38, 40–41, 46–47, 58, 62–103, 112
Jeffs, B.G.F.: 61
Jervis, J.C.: 61
John, *Lt.* von: 36
Jones, H.W.G.: 61
Joyce, Wayland J.: 103
Junginger, Georg: 80, 92
Just, Adolf: 64
Karstedt, ?: 11
Kastner, Hermann: 12, 17–18, 40, 57, 67, 72, 76, 100–101
Kautzsch, Dr.: 84
Keller, Alfred: 24
Kemp, Herbert T.: 72, 85, 103
Kingdon, Leonard: 61
Kirmaier, Stefan: 25, 28, 54–55
Kirsch, Georges: 61
König, Erich: 25, 54–55
Lahmann, Heinrich: 62–63
Laffert, Maximilian von: 74
Lanagan-Byrne, P.A.: 54
LeBas, Owen V.: 85, 103
Leclerc, Gaston: 61
Le Croart, Félix: 61
Leeson, David: 103
Lenz, Alfred: 48
Libman, Jacques: 61
Linde, Otto von der: 18
Loerzer, Fritz: 48
Loviconi, Jacques: 61
Ludwig III, King (Bavaria): 74
Lyncker, Moritz von: 29
Mallinckrodt, Friedrich: 48
Manfield, N.P.: 61
Marie, Duchess (Anhalt): 29
McCubbin, C.R.: 77–78, 80
Meinecke, Emil: 49
Mortimer-Phelan, William C.: 103
Mowat, Morden M.: 103
Müller, Julius: 7, 59
Müller, Max *Ritter* von: 25
Mulzer, Max *Ritter* von: 80–81, 83
Navarre, Jean: 81, 85
Notzke, Werner: 10, 42, 44
Oesterreicher, Albert: 16, 40, 77, 101
Palmer, Charles W.: 103
Parschau, Otto: 10–13, 33, 35, 57–58, 67, 97
Pégoud, Adolphe: 10
Pinder, F.G.: 103
Porr, *Lt.*, 14
Porter, L.: 61
Pritzelwitz, Kurt von: 12
Pulleyn, J.L.: 61
Queri, Georg: 75
Rackow, Kurt: 23

Reid, William: 68, 103
Reimann, Leopold Rudolf: 24–25, 52
Renaud, *Asp.*: 61
Ribiere, Roger: 21–22
Richthofen, Lothar von: 57
Richthofen, Manfred von: 23–28, 54
Ritter, *Hptm.*: 13, 67, 86
Robbins, C.R.: 85
Roberts, C.L.: 61
Robinson, T.N.U.: 77–79
Rogers, Clarence E.: 77
Rupprecht, Crown Prince (Bavaria): 13, 20, 28, 35, 74, 76, 90
Saint, W.B.: 61
Samuels, G.B.: 61
Sander, ?: 11
Savage, John R.B.: 77–79
Scherl, August: 19, 75
Schilling, von: 101
Scott-Brown, William A.: 103
Seckendorf, *Lt.* von: 40
Selter, Chaplain, 29
Sieverts, Ernst: 75, 84–85
Slade, R.J.: 100, 103
Smith, 2Lt.: 61
Somervell, William E.: 61
Stalker, R.M.: 61
Stempel, Friedrich: 81
Störck, *Gefr.*: 72
Strathy, J.M.: 61
Streccius, Hans: 10–11
Sugden-Wilson, W.H.: 100, 103
Swope, Herbert Bayard: 24–25, 31
Taylor, H.: 77
Taylor, H.A.: 61
Tétu, Maurice: 14, 30, 61
Teubern, Erhardt von: 13, 17, 38, 58, 66–67, 86–87
Thomsen, Hermann: 16–17, 22, 29, 48, 72
Tower, H.C.: 61
Tudor-Jones, C.E.G.: 103
Turin, René: 61, 103
Vibert, Gaston: 61
Vivien, Louis: 61
Waller, J.H.: 77–78, 80
Weddigen, Otto: 18
Welsford, G.K.: 61
Welsford, Geoffrey J.L.: 103
Wilcox, W.T.: 61
Wilhelm, Crown Prince (Prussia): 22–23, 58
Wilhelm, Kaiser: 8, 18, 23, 28–29, 50, 72, 76
Wilson, Robert E.: 25, 61
Windisch, Rudolf: 84
Wintgens, Kurt: 25, 58
Wortmann, Hans: 54–55
Wühlisch, Heinz Hellmut von: 13–15, 35, 58

Aviation Units:
Armee-Flug-Park (AFP) 3: 66, 86, 102
Armee-Flug-Park (AFP) 4: 10, 32
Artillerie-Flieger-Abteilung (AFA) 203: 16, 20, 44, 60
Artillerie-Flieger-Abteilung (AFA) 207: 31
Brieftauben-Abteilung Metz (B.A.M.): 16–17, 38, 49, 58, 60, 100
Brieftauben-Abteilung Ostende (B.A.O.): 57
Escadrille C56: 61
Escadrille MF8: 61
Escadrille MF16: 61
Escadrille MF19: 61
Escadrille MF63: 61
Escadrille MS15: 61
Escadrille N15: 61, 103
Escadrille N65: 61
Escadrille VB103: 61
Escadrille VB109: 61
Escadrille VB110: 61
Etappen-Flugzeug-Park 4: 10, 32
Feldflieger-Abteilung (FFA) 5b: 96
Feldflieger-Abteilung (FFA) 6: 49
Feldflieger-Abteilung (FFA) 10: 13, 65–66, 86, 102
Feldflieger-Abteilung (FFA) 13: 10–11, 32, 34, 57, 60
Feldflieger-Abteilung (FFA) 20: 13, 35
Feldflieger-Abteilung (FFA) 24: 66, 69–71, 90, 95
Feldflieger-Abteilung (FFA) 32: 24
Feldflieger-Abteilung (FFA) 62: 8, 12–13, 15–18, 20, 34–36, 38–41, 44, 57, 60, 65–66, 75–77, 86, 88, 90, 96–97, 100, 102
Feld–Luftpark 6b: 92
Flieger-Ersatz-Abteilung (FEA) 2: 66, 86, 102
Flieger-Ersatz-Abteilung (FEA) 3: 10, 60
Fokkerstaffel Jametz: 48
Fokkerstaffel Sivry: 39–40, 48
Jagdstaffel (Jasta) 1: 23–25
Jagdstaffel (Jasta) 2: 23–25, 28, 31, 50–57, 60
Jagdstaffel (Jasta) 4: 25
Jagdstaffel (Jasta) 6: 48
Kampfgeschwader (KG) 2: 23, 30, 77
Kampfstaffel 10: 23
Kampfeinsitzer-Kommando (KEK) 3: 77, 80, 96, 102
Kampfeinsitzer-Kommando (KEK) Avillers: 31
Kampfeinsitzer-Kommando (KEK) Douai: 77, 80, 96, 102
Kampfeinsitzer-Kommando (KEK) Sivry: 20, 42–44, 46, 60
RFC No.2 Squadron: 15, 61, 68, 103
RFC No.3 Squadron: 103
RFC No.4 Squadron: 103
RFC No.5 Squadron: 61
RFC No.7 Squadron: 61
RFC No.8 Squadron: 61, 103
RFC No.10 Squadron: 85, 100, 103
RFC No.11 Squadron: 61, 72, 100, 103
RFC No.12 Squadron: 61
RFC No.15 Squadron: 61, 85, 103
RFC No.16 Squadron: 103
RFC No.21 Squadron: 61
RFC No.22 Squadron: 61
RFC No.23 Squadron: 103
RFC No.24 Squadron: 54, 61
RFC No.25 Squadron: 77
RFC No.32 Squadron: 61
RFC No.45 Squadron: 61
RFC No.60 Squadron: 61
RFC No.70 Squadron: 61

Above: Oswald Boelcke wearing his *Pour le Mérite*.

Bibliography & Glossary

Bibliography
Books
Aschenborn, Willy. "*Als Beobachter Boelckes im Westen*" p.216-17; in Walter von Eberhardt, *Unsere Luftstreitkräfte 1914–18* (Berlin: Verlag C.A. Weller, 1930)

Bronnenkant, Lance. *The Imperial German Eagles in World War I: Their Pictures and Postcards*, Volume 1 (Atglen: Schiffer Publishing, 2006)

Bronnenkant, Lance. *The Imperial German Eagles in World War I: Their Pictures and Postcards*, Volume 2 (Atglen: Schiffer Publishing, 2008)

Bronnenkant, Lance. *The Imperial German Eagles in World War I: Their Pictures and Postcards*, Volume 3 (Atglen: Schiffer Publishing 2011)

Fischer, Suzanne Hayes. *Mother of Eagles* (Atglen: Schiffer Publishing, 2001)

Franks, Norman. *Sharks Among Minnows* (London: Grub Street, 2001)

Frei, Friedrich. *Unser Fliegerheld Immelmann†* (Leipzig: Vogel & Vogel, c.1916)

Gottschalk, Rudolf. *Boelcke† Deutschlands Fliegerheld* (Leipzig: Verlagsanstalt Vogel, c.1917)

Grosz, Peter. *Fokker E.I/II* (Berkhamsted: Albatros Productions, 2002)

Grosz, Peter. *Fokker E.IV* (Berkhamsted: Albatros Publications, 1996)

Grosz, Peter. *The LVG B.I* (Berkhamsted: Albatros Productions, 2003)

Heuer, William. *Held-Immelmann* (Leipzig: Martin Boas Verlag, c.1916)

Immelmann, Franz. *Immelmann, "der Adler von Lille"* (Leipzig: Verlag K.F Koehler, 1942)

Immelmann, Franz (trans. by Claud Sykes). *Immelmann, "The Eagle of Lille"* (London: John Hamilton, unknown)

Immelmann, Max. *Meine Kampfflüge* (Berlin: Verlag August Scherl, 1917)

Kranzler, Wilhelm. *Bezwinger der Luft* (Berlin-Charlottenburg: Verlag der Schillerbuchhandlung, c.1916)

Luebke, Anton. *Hauptmann Boelcke†* (Warendorf: J. Schnellsche Verlagsbuchhandlung, c.1917)

Malkowsky, Emil. *Vom Heldenkampf der deutschen Flieger* (Berlin: Askanischer Verlag, 1916)

O'Connor, Neal. *Aviation Awards of Imperial Germany in World War I and the Men Who Earned Them*, Volume 2. (Princeton: Foundation for WWI Aviation, 1990)

O'Connor, Neal. *Aviation Awards of Imperial Germany in World War I and the Men Who Earned Them*, Volume 6. (Stratford: Flying Machines Press, 1999)

Richthofen, Kunigunde von. *Mein Kriegstagebuch* (Berlin: Verlag Ullstein, 1937)

Richthofen, Manfred von. *Der Rote Kampfflieger* (Berlin: Verlag Ullstein, 1933)

Richthofen, Manfred von. *Ein Heldenleben* (Berlin: Verlag Ullstein, 1920)

Richthofen, Manfred von (trans. by Peter Kilduff). *The Red Baron* (New York: Doubleday, 1969)

Sommer, Rolf. *Fliegerhauptmann Oswald Boelcke. Ein deutsches Heldenleben* (Potsdam: Stiftungsverlag –Potsdam, 1916)

Thies, Andreas. *Auktion Nachlass Oswald Boelcke* (private publication, 2001)

VanWyngarden, Greg. *Early German Aces of World War 1* (New York: Osprey, 2006)

Werner, Prof. Johannes. *Boelcke: der Mensch, der Flieger, der Führer der deutschen Jagdfliegerei* (Leipzig: Verlag K.F. Koehler, 1932)

Werner, Prof. Johannes. *Briefe eines deutschen Kampffliegers an ein junges Mädchen* (Leipzig: Verlag K.F. Koehler, 1930)

Werner, Prof. Johannes (trans. by Claud Sykes). *Knight of Germany: Oswald Boelcke, German Ace* (Novato: Presidio Press, 1991)

_____. *Hauptmann Boelckes Feldberichte* (Gotha: Verlag Friedrich Andreas Perthes, 1916)

Periodicals & Newspapers
Cross & Cockade Journal (U.S.) (Whittier: The Society for WWI Aero Historians) 1962, 1971, 1973
    3:3 "Reminiscences of *Jasta* 10" by H. H. Nowarra
    12:3 "Emil Meinecke. Fighter Ace on the Dardanelles" by Brian Flanagan
    14:2 "A Fighter Pilot on the Western Front"

Die Luftflotte (Berlin: Deutscher Luftflotten-Verein) 1916

Die Woche (Berlin: Verlag August Scherl) 1916

Over The Front (League of WWI Aviation Historians) 1990, 1993, 2002
    5:1 "Many Battles and Many a Bold Adventure: Letters of *Oberleutnant* Erwin Böhme" by Douglas Fant

8:4 "Rebuilding *Jasta* Boelcke, *Leutnant* Erwin Böhme's Letters" by Douglas Fant and *Dr.-Ing.* Niedermeyer
17:3 "A Snapshot of Boelcke" by Lance Bronnenkant
The New York Times (New York: New York Times Co.) 1916

Glossary

Artillerie-Flieger-Abteilung (AFA)	artillery cooperation aviation unit
Armee-Korps	army corps
Armee-Flug-Park (AFP)	army aviation supply depot
Brieftauben-Abteilung (B.A.)	carrier pidgeon unit (code for bombing unit)
Ehrenbecher	honor goblet (usually awarded to airman after 1st victory)
Eindecker	monoplane
Eisenbahn-Regiment	railway regiment
Etappen-Flugzeugpark	army aviation supply depot
Fähnrich	officer candidate
Fahnenjünker	officer candidate, ensign
Feldflieger-Abteilung (FFA)	field aviation unit
Feldflugchef	Chief of Army Field Aviation
Feldwebel (Fw.)	Sergeant
Fliegerbataillon	aviation batallion
Flieger-Ersatz-Abteilung (FEA)	aviation replacement unit
Fokkerstaffel	unit equipped with Eindecker aircraft
Gefreiter (Gefr.)	Private 1st Class
General (Gen.)	General
Grenadier-Regiment	grenadier regiment
Hauptmann (Hptm.)	Captain
Heeresbericht	army reports
Jäger-Bataillon	light infantry batallion
Jagdstaffel (Jasta)	fighter unit
Kampfeinsitzer-Kommando (KEK)	single-seat fighter unit
Kampfgeschwader (KG)	fighting squadron
Kampfstaffel (Kasta)	fighting unit
Kapitänleutnant (Kptlt.)	Captain-Lieutenant (U.S. Navy full Lieutenant)
Leutnant (Lt.)	2nd Lieutenant
Major (Maj.)	Major
Oberleutnant (Oblt.)	1st Lieutenant
Oberleutnant zur See (Oblt.z.See)	Senior Lieutenant (U.S. Navy Lieutenant Junior Grade)
Oberstleutnant (Oberstlt.)	Lieutenant Colonel
Offizierstellvertreter (Offz-Stv.)	Warrant Officer
Staffel	flight section
Telegraphen-Bataillon	wireless batallion

Color Profile Captions

Introduction
Though contemporary documentation is scarce, it is believed that most Fokker monoplanes were covered in plain, unbleached, clear-doped fabric. The linen used was reportedly very coarse and, to judge from photos, relatively opaque. Also, after any appreciable use the inevitable oil staining darkened and soiled the fabric. One of the few available reports on a captured *Eindecker*, from the French periodical *L'aerophile*, stated that "…the fabric of the Fokker wings was generally of beige color in 1916". Another contemporary French eyewitness description[1] reports, "It is a Fokker… his wings are a straw yellow with the cross of Malta."

On the other hand, British ace James T.B. McCudden described one of the first Fokkers he encountered (19 December 1915) as a "…long dark brown form fairly streaking across the sky… I now saw the black crosses on the underneath surface of the Fokker's wings, for a Fokker it was…"[2] While they must be treated with caution, other RFC combat reports mention a range of impressions of Fokker monoplane colors, from "white" to "…a single seater monoplane, with dark brown wings on the upper side."[3] It is certainly likely that some of the later *Eindecker* examples were painted darker in attempts at camouflage (most likely applied by front-line units), but for all of the machines in this volume artist Jim Miller has wisely opted for a deep, opaque beige or light brown representing clear-doped unbleached fabric.

Profile No. 1: Fokker E.IV 123/15
The history and evolving appearance of this machine are well covered by the accompanying photos and text. The fuselage displayed what is believed to have been Boelcke's personal embellishment of a wide white band around the fuselage, and centered on the national iron cross marking. The white band extended onto the top of the fuselage at least, but the national insignia did not. It is unknown if this band extended to the underside of the fuselage as well, but it was important enough to have been repainted at least once in order to cover up the usual staining.[4]

At some point, the wheel covers of this machine were painted in what is believed to have been three equal segments in the German national tricolor of red, white and black. Modelers should also note the interesting stylized "OB" initials in a metal motif attached to the front of the cowling as seen in the photos.

Profile No. 2: Fokker D.III 352/16
Unlike the Fokker monoplanes, many of the early D.II and D.III machines seem to have been covered in a very pale clear-doped fabric, probably bleached linen. The fabric on the wings appears very translucent in many photos, thus leading to the conclusion that it was clear-doped and not painted a pale color. It was evidently light enough that no white-painted background for the national insignia was considered necessary; rather the cross emblems were painted directly on the pale fabric (indeed, the ace Josef Jacobs was so concerned about the 'white' appearance of his Fokker D.II 541/16 that he had it painted "…dark blue, otherwise she would shine and be too visible in the sky"). Here, this bright fabric has been interpreted as a very pale off-white, which nonetheless displayed considerable staining from the twin-row Oberursel engine. The metal engine panels, rear decking and cowlings were given the distinctive 'riffling' so characteristic of early Fokker finishes. After this machine was selected for preservation in a museum, it was apparently completely re-finished by the Fokker factory and given a painted cowling and multi-tone camouflage finish on all upper surfaces; but that was not how it appeared when Boelcke flew it at *Jasta* 2.

Profile No. 3: Albatros D.II 386/16
This aircraft was apparently the Albatros D.II prototype, which was eventually delivered to Boelcke at *Jasta* 2. It was part of the order for 12 Albatros D-type pre-production/prototype aeroplanes ordered near the last part of June 1916, numbered D.380–391/16. Most of these were D.I types but D.386/16 was the first (?) D.II and D.388/16 was a D.III prototype. Of the six new Albatros fighters delivered to *Jasta* 2 on 16 September, five were D.Is and one was this D.II. The fuselage of this machine was left in its varnished plywood finish, but the wings, tailplane/elevators and rudder were camouflaged – apparently in dark olive green, light Brunswick green, and a Venetian red (chestnut brown). In addition, it seems that some of these colors were applied in a densely 'swirled' splotch pattern (possibly with rags or sponges), clearly visible on the rudder and at least part of the lower wing. The late Alex Imrie believed that the rudder was finished with "random brushed blotches" of a reddish-brown stain, but it now seems clear that this was an experimental camouflage application that Albatros applied to several of the D.I's which arrived at *Jasta* 2 as well as on D.386/16. Unfortunately, the precise pattern of camouflage application on the wings cannot be discerned from available photos.

It seems that *Hptm.* Boelcke applied no special markings to this machine, but rather chose to identify it with black-white-red streamers trailing from both lower wingtips. This aircraft also featured a signal pistol tube that protruded from just beneath the left side of the cockpit.[5]

4. Fokker E.I 13/15, Immelmann, *FFA* 62
This aircraft was certainly a significant machine in the history of German fighter aviation, as Immelmann used it to achieve his first victory in a single-seater armed with a forward-firing machine gun on 1 August 1915, as well as his second and third victories. This same machine was flown by Boelcke to give rides to two visiting nurses in the first part of August. Unfortunately for enthusiasts of distinctive colors and markings, E.I 13/15 was very much a "plain plane". Jim Miller's superb profile depicts the airplane as it appeared when Immelmann first flew it, with no national insignia applied to the clear-doped (albeit liberally stained) linen fabric. Most of the military serial number on the fuselage was obliterated by exhaust fumes or removed when the oil stains from the rotary engine were cleaned up. After this machine was badly shot up in a fight on 23 September it underwent some repair work, and it seems likely that the national insignia on a white square panel was applied to the fuselage at that time. It certainly displayed prominent fuselage crosses when it was displayed at Dresden's Royal Saxon Army Museum.

5. Fokker E.II 37/15
Boelcke & Immelmann flew this aircraft at *FFA* 62
This aircraft was first used by Boelcke to attain his third victory on 9 September 1915. However, he did not fly it for long as the 100 hp engine apparently threw a cylinder, severely damaging the cowling and propeller. By the time it was serviceable again (on 8 October), Boelcke had been transferred to *B.A.M.*, and E.II 37/15 was taken over by Immelmann. He was certainly flying it when he attained his 5th victory on 26 October as evidenced by several photos. He also flew it to Lille on 14 November to be feted by Crown Prince Rupprecht of Bavaria, and used it to give a flying display for Saxony's King Friedrich August III at *FFA* 24's airfield the next day. It was there he was photographed in front of E.II 37/15 in a view which became the basis for Sanke postcard S347. Once again, this *Eindecker* displayed only the necessary national markings on a clear-doped linen finish, with no special embellishments.

6. Fokker E.IV 127/15, Immelmann, *FFA* 62
Several good photos provide a look at the appearance of Immelmann's 160 hp E.IV 127/15. Like most of Immelmann's other machines it bore an unremarkable factory finish, displaying only the national insignia. He operated this particular machine for his seventh confirmed success of 2 March 1916 and his two following victories on 10 March. Immelmann also suffered a grimly portentous failure of his guns' synchronizing system in this aircraft in March, but managed to land the aircraft safely despite having sawed both propeller blades off.

7. Fokker E.III 246/16, Immelmann, *KEK* 3
This aircraft's appearance has been reconstructed from the photos of Immelmann's fatal crash, though the only intact portion of the airframe was the aft portion of the fuselage. *Werknummer* 545 was neatly stenciled in black on the upper surfaces of both elevators, on the inside edge next to the rudder post. The rest of the airframe is assumed to have borne only a factory finish as depicted. This was only a reserve machine that Immelmann had been forced to use on his fateful second flight of 18 June 1916. His Fokker E.IV had been put out of service from battle damage suffered during his first flight of the day.

Endnotes:
1. Béraud-Villars, Jean, *Notes d'in pilote disparu,* 1918.
2. McCudden, J.T.B., *Five Years in the Royal Flying Corps*, 1918.
3. Gray, B.J., "The Anatomy of an Aeroplane; The DeHavilland DH2 Pusher Scout," *Cross & Cockade International Journal*, Vol. 22 No. 4, 1991, p.198.
4. The late historian Alex Imrie was of the opinion that the wide white fuselage band was a unit marking frequently employed on aircraft of *B.A.M.* and that this was the origin of this marking on Boelcke's Fokker E.IV. However, the timing of the arrival of E.IV 123/15 at *FFA* 62 makes this somewhat unlikely.
5. Many readers will be familiar with references to "Boelcke's black machine" which sometimes turn up in WWI literature. There was a widely-held, if erroneous, belief among French airmen – and their American comrades of the 'Lafayette Escadrille' – that Boelcke flew a largely black Fokker *Eindecker*; this rumor seems to have spread to British airmen also. "Bert" Hall of the 'Lafayette' wrote: 'I encountered Captain Boelke (sic)... He had a Fokker fighter which was painted black with white crosses." Victor Chapman was almost certainly wounded by Boelcke on 17 June 1916, and he also described his opponent as flying a black Fokker. The New York Times article of 21 printed here goes further, reporting that Chapman stated, "His assailant was flying a black machine which coincides with American accounts of Boelke (sic)... Americans say that Boelke's (sic) aeroplane is black with a huge skull under each wing." In spite of such contemporary impressions, there is absolutely no photographic evidence or contemporary German accounts that indicate such a black machine existed. The 18 June Times article describing Boelcke's combat with Roger Ribiere describes a "Fokker painted yellow", which is much closer to the actual appearance of Boelcke's various Fokker monoplanes.